COVENT CATHEDRAL

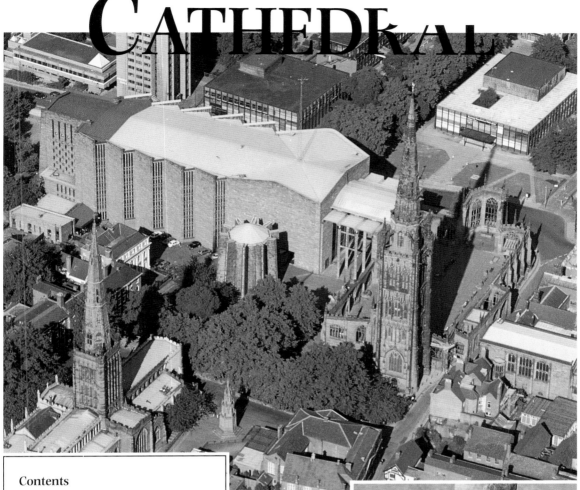

Contents

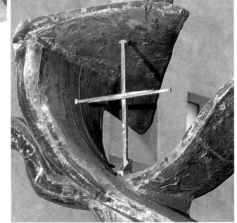

Above:
Coventry Cathedral old and new in its urban setting. In the foreground, Holy Trinity Church.

Right:
The original Cross of Nails, symbol of reconciliation, set within the high altar cross.

The Provost's Welcome

Welcome to Coventry Cathedral.

To move from the bombed ruins into the new cathedral building is to walk from Good Friday to Easter, from death to new life, from the jagged reminder of man's inhumanity to the soaring architecture that lifts the heart. I hope that, along with me, you want to say 'Thank God'.

Many people from abroad still tell us that coming to the cathedral is the most memorable experience of their time in this country. My hope is that this guide, which aims to interpret that experience, may help to turn each visitor into a pilgrim.

God bless you on your journey.

THE PROVOST

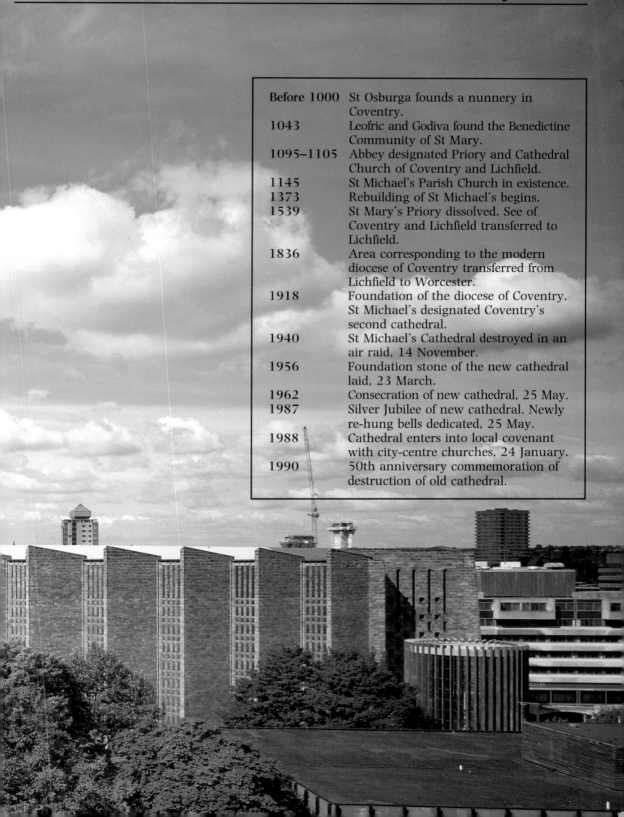

History Chart

Before 1000	St Osburga founds a nunnery in Coventry.
1043	Leofric and Godiva found the Benedictine Community of St Mary.
1095–1105	Abbey designated Priory and Cathedral Church of Coventry and Lichfield.
1145	St Michael's Parish Church in existence.
1373	Rebuilding of St Michael's begins.
1539	St Mary's Priory dissolved. See of Coventry and Lichfield transferred to Lichfield.
1836	Area corresponding to the modern diocese of Coventry transferred from Lichfield to Worcester.
1918	Foundation of the diocese of Coventry. St Michael's designated Coventry's second cathedral.
1940	St Michael's Cathedral destroyed in an air raid, 14 November.
1956	Foundation stone of the new cathedral laid, 23 March.
1962	Consecration of new cathedral, 25 May.
1987	Silver Jubilee of new cathedral. Newly re-hung bells dedicated, 25 May.
1988	Cathedral enters into local covenant with city-centre churches, 24 January.
1990	50th anniversary commemoration of destruction of old cathedral.

'To the Glory of God this Cathedral Burnt'

To stand in the ruins of the old Coventry Cathedral is to stand in one of the most evocative places in England. For people from all over the world, the remains of that building, its noble tower and spire still standing proud on the skyline of a modern industrial city, are an unforgettably poignant reminder of our human condition. They speak not only of what the poet Wilfred Owen called 'the pity of war', but also of the inescapable issues that face us all as individual men and women or as peoples and communities. They speak of life, of death, of destiny. The ruins, open to the sky, are like a place of martyrdom – to quote Nikolaus Pevsner, a place in which to ponder life's ultimate questions.

But alongside, its great porch overarching, embracing almost, the place of destruction, rises the new building. And as we are drawn towards it, we begin to grasp the fact that these are not two cathedrals but one, a single statement of faith in the gospel story of death and resurrection. That is why the proper place to begin a visit to Coventry Cathedral is in the ruins, for they are an anteroom to the splendour of the new cathedral as surely as Good Friday prepares for Easter. Coventry Cathedral stands as a sign that this movement from Good Friday to Easter embraces all of human life. It is an icon of a suffering God, through whose death and resurrection come life, light and love.

Above: (11)
Christ crucified. Helen Jennings's sculpture, created out of a wrecked motor car, is seen against the baptistry window: suffering transfigured into glory.

Right: (2)
Blossom frames the porch linking the old cathedral to the new.

Left: (1)
Two days after its destruction, King George VI visited Coventry. He expressed 'intense sympathy and grief,' recalled Provost Howard, seen here in the cathedral ruins with the King.

1,000 Casualties in Coventry Attack

SEVERE DAMAGE TO CITY

"Blitzkrieg" Raid on Midlands

CATHEDRAL AMONG THE BUILDINGS HIT

LONDON, Friday.

THE city of Coventry was heavil the scale of the raids being of the largest night attacks on L try of Home Security.

THE ENEMY PLANE ᴇᴅ BY INTENSIᴠ ᴇᴘᴛ T

Horror Beyond Words

Coventry, Pile of Rubble

Thousands Lose Homes, But Spirit Unbroken

Australian Associated Press

LONDON, Sat

press corres- ntry yesterday big that indi.

SAVAGE AIR RAID ON COVENTRY.

— ◆ —

Casualties Near 1,000.

CATHEDRAL DESTROYED

Left:
Contemporary news coverage of the Coventry air raid which stunned the nation.

Below:
A symbol of Christ suffering with his people: the burnt out cathedral ruins, with the two fallen roof-timbers suggesting the shape of a cross.

Most of the great ruined churches of England are the outcome of the violence of an earlier age, the dissolution of the monasteries. But the ruins of St Michael's Church are the consequence of the violence of modern times. On the night of Thursday, 14 November 1940, the Luftwaffe headed for Coventry in what was codenamed 'Operation Moonlight Sonata'. The raid devastated the city. And as it burned, its cathedral burned with it. A total of 568 people lost their lives. Many more would die in subsequent air raids on British cities, to say nothing of the hundreds of thousands who would do so in Allied air raids on German cities such as Dresden. But the raid on Coventry proved particularly poignant for two reasons. For one thing, it was the first British city to suffer in this way. So significant was this that the Luftwaffe coined a new word to describe the wholesale destruction of cities, *zu Coventrieren* – 'to coventrate'. And secondly, Coventry was the only British city to lose its cathedral as a result of aerial bombardment. For a city to lose its cathedral is, perhaps, somehow, for it to lose its soul.

It would not have been surprising if, following the raid, another kind of flame were to have been fanned into being – the fire of bitterness and hatred. It was largely due to the inspired, prophetic leadership of the Provost at that time, Dick Howard, that a different spirit prevailed. On the morning after its destruction, the resolve to rebuild the cathedral was born, not as an act of defiance, but rather as a sign of faith, trust, and hope for the future of the world. Shortly afterwards, the cathedral's stonemason, Jock Forbes, observing that two of the charred medieval roof timbers had fallen across each other amid the rubble, tied them together, and set them up in the ruined sanctuary. Again it was the imagination of Provost Howard that led to the words 'Father, forgive' being inscribed behind the charred cross. At the same time, a local priest, the Revd Arthur Wales, created another cross by binding together three of the huge medieval nails that littered the debris. This Cross of Nails, which has become the symbol of Coventry's international ministry of reconciliation, was also placed in the ruined sanctuary, on a simple stone altar, built there as an 'altar of reconciliation'.

The profound eloquence of the ruins is not, then, simply architectural. It is the story they tell that gives them their meaning, their peculiarly redemptive power, their ability gently to heal memories, bearing witness to the deep truth of the words they hold at their heart, 'Father, forgive'.

'Built Half-way to the Sky'

Coventry's three spires have for centuries been a famous sight. Even today, as you hurtle towards the city from the east, along the busy A45, and drop down from the higher ground called Dunsmore, that same view opens up before you — despite the seemingly relentless encroachments of glass and concrete rectangles upon a beautiful skyline.

Once upon a time, however, you would have seen no less than six spires rising above the city. For alongside the magnificent parish churches of St Michael and Holy Trinity, and older than either of them, once stood Coventry's earliest cathedral, dedicated to St Mary. It was founded as a Benedictine community by Leofric, Earl of Mercia, and his wife Godiva in 1043 on the site, it is thought, of a still earlier religious house for nuns, established before the 10th century. Something of its grandeur is hinted at by the scant remains that can be seen alongside the Visitors' Centre entrance to

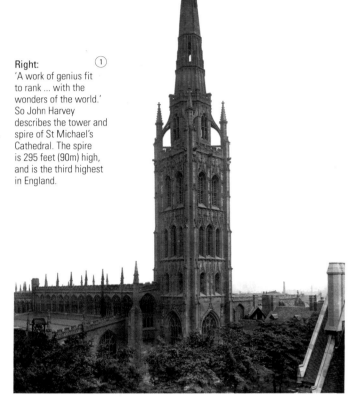

Right: ①
'A work of genius fit to rank ... with the wonders of the world.' So John Harvey describes the tower and spire of St Michael's Cathedral. The spire is 295 feet (90m) high, and is the third highest in England.

Left:
The three spires of Coventry, depicted in an 18th-century print. From left to right: the church of the Greyfriars (Christ Church, destroyed in 1940), Holy Trinity, and St Michael's.

the undercroft of the new cathedral. Probably one of the great religious buildings of medieval England, its sheer size is some indication of the wealth which Coventry acquired in the Middle Ages as the fourth city in England after London, Bristol and York.

With the dissolution of the monasteries in 1539, the See of Coventry and Lichfield was transferred to Lichfield, whereupon Leofric and Godiva's priory church fell into decay. Only in 1918 was the modern diocese of Coventry created in its own right, and St Michael's designated its cathedral.

Above: ①
The polygonal apse of St Michael's, with the altar of reconciliation and charred cross.

Above inset: ①
Prayers of penitence and reconciliation are said in the ruins each Friday at noon. The Communion is celebrated there at dawn on Easter Day and Whitsunday.

The church, built virtually throughout in the Perpendicular style, represented a considerable enlargement of an earlier building. The rebuilding was begun in 1373, and completed by about 1460. The tower, with its wealth of decoration, together with its spire supported by flying buttresses, miraculously escaped destruction in 1940. Its twelve bells were rehung for the cathedral's Silver Jubilee celebrations in 1987, and now ring again after a century's silence.

The ruins remain consecrated ground, symbolized not only by the altar of reconciliation, but also by the 'hallowing places' around its walls, engraved plaques focusing on different aspects of human achievement and endeavour, a modern interpretation of the medieval guild chapels that once lined the nave of St Michael's and spoke of the offering of all of human life to God. It was precisely that understanding of life that led to the vision of the new cathedral.

The Phoenix Rises

The decision to rebuild Coventry Cathedral was taken on the morning after its destruction in 1940. It was, however, to be 15 years before the work of reconstruction could begin. An initial design for a new cathedral, submitted by Sir Giles Gilbert Scott, architect of the Anglican cathedral at Liverpool, was dropped. The design was then thrown open to competition, and 219 architects submitted plans.

The winner, Basil Spence (1907–1976), who was later knighted for his achievement at Coventry, tells us of his experience of first setting foot in the cathedral ruins. 'I was deeply moved. I saw the old cathedral as standing clearly for the Sacrifice, one side of the Christian Faith, and I knew my task was to design a new one which would stand for the Triumph of the Resurrection ... In these few moments the idea of the design was planted. In essence it has never changed.'

The foundation stone was laid by HM

Above right:
Basil Spence's 1951 vision of the cathedral: 'a great nave and an altar ... and a huge picture behind it'.

Right:
Spence's book, *Phoenix at Coventry*, gives a unique insight into the creation of a great work of architecture. In this photograph, the saw-tooth nave walls are already defined, with the foundations of the Chapel of Unity alongside.

The Queen on 23 March 1956, by which time work had already been in progress for a year. John Laing & Co were the main contractors. From the first, the immense project captured the imagination of donors all over the world. Gifts arrived from Germany, Canada, Hong Kong, Sweden and other countries, as well as from Coventry itself and the surrounding area, both to commission the works of art which were to fill the cathedral, and also to endow its future ministry. The cathedral was, in terms of the quality of its craftsmanship, to prove a remarkable achievement, a treasure house of some of the best artistic talent of its time. Meanwhile, the rhythms of cathedral life went on. Special services continued to be held in the ruined nave. Underneath, two crypt chapels had been spared destruction, and in them the worship of the cathedral was maintained. The Bishop's throne, or *cathedra*, was placed in the tiny Wyley Chapel, while, next to it, in what is now called the Chapel of the Cross, the cathedral congregation met Sunday by Sunday until 1958, when the undercroft of the new cathedral was completed.

On 25 May 1962, in the presence of HM The Queen, the new Cathedral Church of St Michael, Coventry, was consecrated.

Above:
Scaffolding sheathes the immense opening at the west end of the nave, to be filled by John Hutton's glass screen.

Right:
HM The Queen at the service of consecration on 25 May 1962. The consecration was performed by the Bishop of Coventry, Cuthbert Bardsley. The Archbishop of Canterbury preached on the text 'The latter glory of this house shall be greater than the former' (Haggai 2:9).

Above:
Amongst works commissioned for the new cathedral was Benjamin Britten's *War Requiem*, first performed here on 30 May 1962.

Cathedral of the Twentieth Century

The new cathedral stands at right angles to the old, on a north-south axis. Faced with the same rose-red local sandstone, the exterior rises with almost elemental simplicity from its surroundings. Its walls, largely plain and unadorned, have something of the aspect of cliff faces about them. A huge Mercia Cross is the only decoration on the uncompromising wall which towers above the pedestrianized square to the north. From across Priory Street, too, in front of Coventry University, the sheer mass of the building can be appreciated. From here, you see how the great arc of the baptistry window and the saw-tooth profile of the nave wall impart energy and movement into the lines of the building. From here, too, the circular Chapel of Christ the Servant is seen well: its clear glass, an image of the cathedral's worship and mission thrust out into the life of the city, transparent to, and penetrated by, human struggles and concerns. On the other side of the cathedral, the Chapel of Unity makes a similar thrust outwards in the form of another circular structure whose green Westmorland slate offers a fine foil for the red sandstone environment that surrounds it.

Elemental, too, is the great porch. Sir Basil Spence's original designs for the cathedral show a more modest porch, more a passageway between the old and new cathedrals than a place in its own right. The architect was surely right to think, instead, of a mighty canopy, holding the two buildings together in a massive statement of death and resurrection. The St Michael's steps, leading up to the porch, reinforce the air of the dramatic, suggesting a stage at the top; and indeed, this space is often used for ceremonial events. The ensemble is completed by Sir Jacob Epstein's cast bronze sculpture of St Michael and the Devil.

Finally, it is worth noticing the slender aluminium flèche on the cathedral roof. The abstract bronze cross which surmounts it was designed by Geoffrey Clarke. Perhaps more than any other part of the building, this flèche, which anywhere else could be mistaken for a piece of telecommunications hardware, reflects the spirit of the technological age that gave birth to the cathedral, an appropriate image for a church set in a modern, industrial, city.

Right:
Ruined and rebuilt: the cathedral from Priory Street, with the ruined sanctuary behind.

Below: ②
The porch, with Epstein's sculpture of *St Michael and the Devil*. The Ship's Company of HMS *Coventry* is on parade.

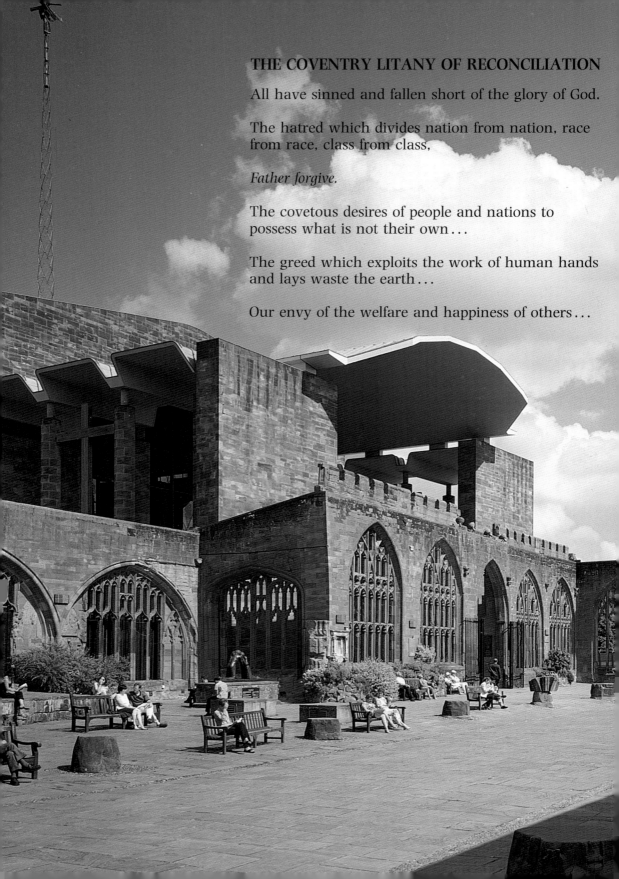

THE COVENTRY LITANY OF RECONCILIATION

All have sinned and fallen short of the glory of God.

The hatred which divides nation from nation, race from race, class from class,

Father forgive.

The covetous desires of people and nations to possess what is not their own...

The greed which exploits the work of human hands and lays waste the earth...

Our envy of the welfare and happiness of others...

Our indifference to the plight of the imprisoned,
the homeless, the refugee…

The lust which dishonours the bodies of men,
women and children…

The pride which leads us to trust in ourselves
and not in God,

Father forgive.

Be kind to one another, tenderhearted, forgiving
one another, as God in Christ forgave you.

Above: ①
Ecce Homo by Sir
Jacob Epstein. The
monumental depiction
of Christ before Pilate
dates from 1934–35.

Left: ①
The ruins are an
international focus of
prayer for reconciliation
and world peace,
including the Statue of
Reconciliation and the
national memorial to
those who served on the
Home Front in the
Second World War.
The Coventry Litany
of Reconciliation is a
prayer based on the
seven deadly sins.

A Theatre for Worship

'The Cathedral should be built to enshrine the altar. This should be the ideal of the architect, not to conceive a building and to place in it an altar, but to conceive an altar, and to create a building. In the Anglican liturgy it is the people's altar; it should offer access for worship and invitation to Communion.'

It was with these words that the competition rules concerning the design of the new cathedral were introduced.

A church is a kind of theatre, in which the drama of the liturgy, the church's worship, is acted out. Like the theatre, it may take different forms. You can have 'traditional' theatre with a proscenium arch, dividing audience from stage. Or you can have 'theatre in the round' in which the audience surrounds the performers, and the distinction between 'stage' and 'auditorium' becomes meaningless. Many modern places of worship have adopted that understanding of liturgy, for example, Liverpool's Roman Catholic cathedral, a circular building with an altar at its centre, surrounded by the congregation.

On entering the nave of Coventry Cathedral, however, we see at once that, as a space for worship, the building is organized along traditional lines, with the high altar towards the east end, separated from the congregation by a chancel in which the choir and ministers perform their duties. In this, it is no different from the great medieval cathedrals where the high altar is, in every sense, the climax of the building.

Right: ⑧
Christ in glory, depicted in Graham Sutherland's immense tapestry, presides over the worship of the cathedral community.

Below: ⑨
The Eucharist, celebrated at the high altar, is the church's central act of worship. The vestments are by John Piper.

16

The high altar, then, is the focus of the cathedral: and the eye is drawn to it immediately by the immense tapestry that forms its backdrop or reredos. Because of the brilliance of the colour on the tapestry, the high altar is, unusually, made to stand out, not by decoration but by sheer starkness. It is, in fact, no more than a huge table of hammered concrete, strong, simple and primitive, reflecting so well the Christian Eucharist that is as old as the Church itself.

The place of baptism, too, like the altar, is given special prominence. At Coventry, the font, like the altar, has its own coloured backdrop – in this case a brilliant array of stained glass. It too has a stark simplicity about it. It consists of a boulder, brought from a hillside near Bethlehem, hollowed out to contain the water for baptism. And from its position near the west end, we see that the entire space of the cathedral is, as it were, poised in a movement between the baptistry at one end and the high altar at the other.

Perhaps, then, we are wrong to describe Coventry Cathedral as 'modern'. The nave piers, and the vault, for example, while undeniably interpreted in new and creative ways, are nevertheless a conscious reworking of the Gothic style. It is no disparagement of a great work of architecture to say that Coventry is perhaps one of the last of the old cathedrals, rather than the first of the new.

Right:
A baptism at the font. The rough 3-ton boulder from Bethlehem has a scallop-shaped bowl hollowed out by Ralph Beyer.

(4)

The cathedral is not, in fact, a large one, but the architect has succeeded in creating the illusion of size by the skilful interplay of distances, perspectives and a fine sense of scale. The roughcast nave walls, rising sheer and cliff-like inside as well as out, convey a sense of height in excess of their actual 70 feet (22m). The vault enhances this effect of height still further. Like the medieval Gothic vaults which it emulates, the effect is of a canopy of branches and leaves in a forest of tall, slender trees.

The west screen is essential to our understanding of the building. From outside, in the porch, the entire nave is open to view through this immense window: if the light is right, the reflections of the ruins behind you make a thought-provoking interplay with the tapestry at

Right: ③
The Angel of the Resurrection from the lowest row in the west screen, which depicts New Testament angels.

Far right: ④
The baptistry window, designed by John Piper and executed by Patrick Reyntiens. It contains 195 panels of brilliantly coloured glass.

Below: ③
The engraving in the west screen is by John Hutton. It depicts angels and saints, including figures from the history of the British Church.

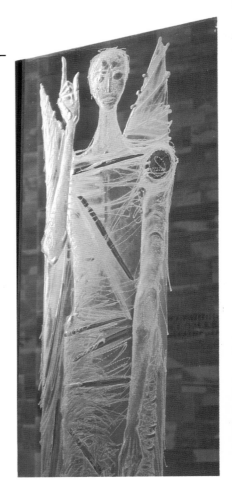

the far end. The old and new buildings are, as we have seen, a single cathedral, and this is what the screen represents: not a west wall to divide them, but an opening to unite them. To the worshipper inside, the message is that worship is not an end in itself; rather, it is open to the world and its concerns, and issues in mission, and the service of our fellow human beings.

The baptistry window is regarded by many as one of the greatest stained-glass windows in the country. The rite of baptism includes the giving of a lighted candle to the newly baptized person as a sign of the light of the risen life of Christ breaking into our human life. This is one way of reading the baptistry window, with its colours moving from darker reds, blues and greens at the periphery to the brilliant sunburst of white and gold at the centre.

The Gathering Place

Looking beyond the altar to the tapestry, the immense figure of Christ sits (although the posture is somewhat ambiguous – deliberately) as a Byzantine Christ Pantocrator, ruling the universe and enthroned in glory, his hands raised in 'blessing, helping ... drawing humanity up into himself', as Provost Howard put it. Around him are the traditional symbols of the four evangelists, drawn from the Old and New Testaments; from his side Satan is thrown down into hell and between his feet stands the figure of a human being. There is triumph here; dominating the cathedral as it does, the tapestry sums up the entire message of the building. But this is not triumphalism, the brash assertion of victory without cost, struggle or pain. The hands and feet of Christ carry the marks of the nails of crucifixion. He wears not so much the royal apparel of a king as the robe of a priest. Above all, his face, to which your eye always returns, conveys the message that this Christ is for ever one of us, sharing our human condition.

The tapestry, which replaces the traditional east window, was designed by Graham Sutherland, and woven in France by Pinton Frères at Felletin. It measures 74 feet by 38 feet (23m x 12m), weighs over a ton and at the time of its hanging was the largest tapestry in the world.

From a distance the tapestry looks deceptively like a painting, perhaps an immense fresco. This indeed is how it began life, for it was woven as an exact reproduction of a painted cartoon, photographically enlarged. Sutherland's paintings, both in the cathedral undercroft and in the Herbert Art Gallery, offer a fascinating insight into the long and complex process by which he arrived at the magnificent and moving tapestry we now see.

The word 'nave' means 'ship', for, in the traditional imagery, the church is the

Left: ③
Amid the angels in the west screen, the glass doors contain cherub-handles, finely carved by Sir Jacob Epstein.

Below: ③
The west end of the nave at the enthronement of the Bishop of Coventry, 4 January 1986.

try, are by Ralph Beyer. Beyond them we come to a brass maple leaf that commemorates the gifts made by the people of Canada towards the rebuilding of the cathedral; and, still in the floor, we find a bronze Chi-Ro monogram, an ancient Christian symbol derived from the first two letters of the Greek title 'Christos' – Christ.

The nave floor contains other elements worth noticing, for instance the fossils in the polished marble; and the pennies, dated 1962 but now mostly worn flat by the footfalls of millions of visitors, that mark processional ways for choir and clergy.

place where those who are on a voyage gather together. So the area in front of the west screen, which is usually free of chairs, is a gathering place, and also a place from which people leave after worship. It stands for the movement inwards and outwards that is the heartbeat of Christian living: a movement *in* for worship, fellowship and celebration; a movement *out* for service, mission, and involvement in the life of our fellow human beings.

On the floor of this space is set the inscription: TO THE GLORY OF GOD + THIS CATHEDRAL BURNT NOVEMBER 14 AD 1940 IS NOW REBUILT + 1962. The brass letters, like much of the other lettering to be found at Coven-

Above: (10)
On Easter Eve, worshippers gather in the darkened nave to greet the light of the risen Christ.

Above right: (3)
The maple leaf, in the nave floor. Two feet in width, it was made by Caroline Brown.

Right: (8)
The head of Christ from the tapestry, lit by 'light unapproachable' from above.

'A House of Prayer...'

At the front of the nave, and raised up from it by three gently curving steps, is the part of the cathedral known as the chancel. Its function is signalled by the great lectern and pulpit that stand, like sentinels, on either side of the chancel steps. These were designed in Sir Basil Spence's office by Anthony Blee. The lectern, on the right, is the place from which the Scriptures are publicly read, while the pulpit opposite is the place from which they are interpreted, and their message heard for today's world. So the chancel is a space set apart for the ministry of the word of God. Here are stalls for choir and clergy; here, for the most part, the daily prayers of the cathedral community are said or sung. We saw earlier that Leofric and Godiva's first cathedral was a Benedictine foundation. Common to all communities following the great Rule of St Benedict (c. AD 540) was, and is, the discipline of daily prayer.

Left: ⑩
The bronze eagle on the great lectern is the work of Dame Elisabeth Frink, as is the crucifix on the pulpit opposite.

Here at Coventry Cathedral, the community continues in that Benedictine tradition by coming together each day to celebrate the offices of morning, midday and evening prayer. This rhythm of daily worship is the heartbeat of the cathedral's life.

The canopies above the canons' stalls suggest thorns, or birds in flight. These tower up above the Provost's stall on the right, culminating in a flame, the symbol of the Holy Spirit; and above the Bishop's *cathedra* or throne, left, crowned by a mitre.

Left: (5)
The Tablets of the Word by Ralph Beyer. The uneven lettering of these basic New Testament texts recalls the primitive inscriptions on the walls of the catacombs. Beyond is the organ, by Harrison of Durham.

Right: (9)
Looking down the nave from behind the high altar. Geoffrey Clarke's gilded silver cross is an abstract interpretation of the charred cross in the ruins.

If we now turn and look down the nave from the east end, we see what was quite hidden from view on entering the cathedral at the west end. The ten superb nave windows are orientated eastwards, so as to throw their light towards the high altar. The windows in their colouring represent the same human and religious journey that we have encountered before, linking as they do the place of beginnings, the font, with the place of fulfilment, the high altar. It is integral to Sir Basil Spence's design of the cathedral that these windows, unfolding one by one as you move east up the nave, can only fully be seen as a series by the worshipper returning from the altar rail at Communion.

Left: (5)
Panels from the nave windows, the work of Lawrence Lee, Keith New and Geoffrey Clarke. 70 feet (22m) high, the windows tell the story of human growth from birth through maturity and death to fulfilment, epitomized in the life of Jesus.

23

'...For All People'

The nave of the cathedral is a unity. It has a single focus: the high altar, around which the building has been created as a single, glorious room, reflecting the New Testament conviction that Christians are one people breaking one bread around one altar.

Nevertheless, there is a need for spaces that are more intimate, in which smaller groups of people, or individuals, can worship, meditate and pray.

Approaching the east end by way of the south aisle (the baptistry side), the first chapel we come to is the Chapel of Christ in Gethsemane, its light beckoning from beneath the organ pipes. On drawing near, we find this little chapel to be

an almost cave-like recess, a welcome contrast to the exhilarating, but nevertheless demanding, sense of exposure you find in the nave. Gethsemane means 'the place of pressure'. In the Gospels, Jesus struggles there with his impending suffering and death. The reserved sacrament is kept in this chapel and it is set apart as a place for private prayer, particularly for those who, in their own lives, are experiencing pressure or pain of any kind.

To the right, along a passageway, we come to the Chapel of Christ the Servant. Also known as the Chapel of Industry, its circle of clear glass allows worshippers the sights (and sounds) of the world out-

Below: ⑦
The Gethsemane Chapel. The mosaic of the Angel of Agony by Steven Sykes, seen through the wrought-iron crown of thorns designed by Basil Spence, and made as the gift of the Royal Engineers.

side, another reminder that worship and life belong together. The oils of healing are kept in the chapel, in full view of those who pass up and down Priory Street, as a sign of the church's ministry of healing in the world.

Behind the high altar is the Lady Chapel. In this oblong place, it is hard not to be completely overwhelmed by the immense height of the tapestry above, even though the lower part of the tapestry forms a reredos specifically for this chapel. It depicts the crucifixion of a Christ who is very dead – in striking contrast to the Christ in glory, so much alive, above. The sculpture of Our Lady is by John Bridgeman.

Above right: (6)
The Chapel of Christ the Servant. Around the plinth are inscribed the words 'I AM AMONG YOU AS ONE THAT SERVES'.

Right: (8)
The Swedish windows are by Einar Forseth. Here, St Sigfrid, an 11th-century English missionary to Sweden, tramples on the hammer of Thor.

Below right: (6)
In the Chapel of Christ the Servant, four new canons are admitted by the Bishop to the Cathedral Chapter, prior to their installation at a cathedral service.

Near the west end is the Chapel of Unity, which, like the Chapel of Christ the Servant, is circular, shaped like a tent. Dedicated to the unity of all Christians, the Chapel of Unity reflects a vision of reconciliation that goes back to the days following the destruction of Coventry in 1940. It is not in fact legally part of the cathedral at all, being administered by a Joint Council representing all the mainline Christian denominations in the Coventry area. As you leave the Chapel of Unity, the baptistry window shines opposite, a reminder that whatever their divisions, Christians are united in baptism. The cathedral, along with the other

Right: (11)
Midday Prayer in the Chapel of Unity. Prayers for reconciliation and peace, as well as for Christian unity, are said here each day.

Below: (11)
The Chapel of Unity. Einar Forseth's mosaic floor was the gift of the people of Sweden. Margaret Traherne's glass was given by Christians in Germany.

churches of the city centre, entered a local covenant in 1988 that pledged it, and them, to work ever more closely in the pursuit of a common service and mission. The tasks of reconciliation remain as central to the cathedral's work now as they were in 1940, as does the prayer of Jesus inscribed in the floor at the entrance to the Chapel of Unity: 'THAT THEY MAY ALL BE ONE'.

But a cathedral is more than a place in which to hold services. It embodies community, for it is made up of people. The undercroft is perhaps the expression of all this within the new cathedral itself. Here are the Visitors' Centre, reception rooms, including the Navy Room, furnished as a gift from the Royal Navy, lecture hall, song school for the choir, common room, broadcasting studio, restaurant and shop. All play a part in contributing to the sense of community and hospitality so basic to the ideal of St Benedict that inspired Leofric and Godiva to build their first abbey church 960 years ago.

'New Lamps be Lit, New Tasks Begun'

What is it all *for*?

A cathedral is many things: a great church in its own right, a mother church to its diocese, a place for pilgrims. Coventry Cathedral is all these; and we have seen how the whole building is designed to be a vivid statement of the gospel of Jesus Christ. To that end, the cathedral has never been afraid of pioneering new forms of worship, new patterns of ministry, new ways of serving the human family that will communicate the love of God more effectively in our early 21st-century world. It is a workshop; a place of experiment; a laboratory of the Spirit.

This forward and outward-looking approach to the role of a cathedral began in 1940, when it began to proclaim a ministry of reconciliation; as Provost Bill Williams put it later, 'to say and do something about the situation of division and hatred which accompanied the destruction of the city and the cathedral'. The International Centre in the ruins was opened in 1960 by the Bishop of Berlin, Otto Dibelius, having been furnished by a Berlin donor who had himself lost his entire family in an Allied air raid. The centre was subsequently extended by young volunteer Christians from Germany, the name of whose

Above:
HM The Queen Mother, with the President of Germany, in the ruins on the 50th anniversary of the Coventry Blitz.

Below:
The cathedral youth group helping at a hospital for the mentally handicapped.

organisation, *Aktion Sühnezeichen*, Action Reconciliation, sums up so much of what the early days of the cathedral's life stood for then and continues to represent today.

The ministry of international reconciliation is, perhaps, the unique contribution that Coventry Cathedral, because of its story, has been able to make to church life in these islands and beyond. The Community of the Cross of Nails was founded as a practical expression of the work of reconciliation, supporting the rebuilding of a hospital wing in Dresden, the building of the House of Reconciliation in Corrymeela, Northern Ireland, and a house for friendship and dialogue between Jewish, Christian and Muslim people in Galilee. The cathedral continues to be actively involved in areas of conflict such as Northern Ireland and Central America, while groups, inspired by the symbol of the Cross of Nails, have sprung up in many parts of the world where they, too, work for reconciliation, justice and peace.

Meanwhile, the cathedral seeks to come to terms with what reconciliation means in Coventry in the first decade of the 21st century, for example in the areas of urban deprivation, relations between those of different races and cultures and concern for the environment and the future of our planet. In all three areas, the cathedral has attempted, under the sign of the Cross of Nails, to wrestle with what a Christian response might be, and then to pledge time, money and human resources into making that response a reality. John F. Kennedy spoke about 'making God's work our own'. That is why Coventry Cathedral exists.

Above: ⑮
Summer in the cathedral precinct. The peace pole contains a prayer for peace in four languages.

Left:
The 50th anniversary of the Blitz, 14 November 1990, was marked by a service of remembrance and reconciliation. HM The Queen Mother presented the President of Germany with a Cross of Nails, while the President presented a peace bell.

BRITAIN'S NEW ROYALS

CHAPTER 1

A new generation of British royals

Britain's new royals are the grandchildren and great-grandchildren of Queen Elizabeth II who, led by the UK's future king Prince William, have been at the forefront of a sustained period of elevated popularity for the British monarchy. The senior members of this new generation share a remarkable story, having grown up in the midst of a difficult time for the royal family in the 1990s as a series of controversies and scandals left its reputation in tatters. They were then forced to deal with the death of Princess Diana, her sons princes William and Harry left devastated by the loss of their mother.

What has perhaps endeared the group to the British public so much is the way in which they've recovered from such strife

and tragedy to play their own vital roles in the rebuilding of the royal family in the new millennium. Never was this more evident than in 2011 as the wedding of Prince William and Kate Middleton – who became the Duchess of Cambridge – drew huge worldwide television audiences and saw more than a million people descend on London in celebration. The arrival of their first son, Prince George, in 2013 generated similar interest across the globe.

As these young royals come of age, they play an ever more important part in the affairs of state and have each branched out to pursue their own interests and causes. And it seems whatever they take on, their popularity continues to grow.

Prince William and the Duchess of Cambridge arrive by carriage for the second day of the Royal Ascot horse races meeting, June 15, 2016. AG

Preface

A s a writer and journalist I take great care to avoid clichés, but the truth behind some of our most widely used phrases is hard to dispute. Here's one example: a picture paints a thousand words. An overused idiom maybe, but one that cannot really be argued with, and the 132 pages which make up this volume are surely proof of that.

Through more than 300 carefully selected images, I have endeavoured to tell the story of the new generation of the British royal family starting in the late 1970s when Queen Elizabeth II welcomed her first grandchild Peter Phillips, through to the events of 2016.

It's been a remarkable tale that's unfolded during those nearly 40 years as the young royals have grown up in the spotlight of the world's media, and then started families of their own under the same intense glare.

As sons of the direct heir to the throne, princes William and Harry have been at the forefront and have been the young royals who have taken on the greatest degree of responsibility for official duties. More so, the way in which they have come of age following the tragic and untimely loss of their mother Princess Diana has endeared them to the British public both young and old. Prince William's wife Kate Middleton has captured hearts too, the glamourous young woman becoming a royal princess in a fairy story worthy of Walt Disney.

Then there is the supporting cast; William and Harry's cousins who have, in various ways, forged successful lives and careers both in and out of the public eye.

They, together with their children and spouses, make up Britain's New Royals and I sincerely hope that you enjoy this insight into their life and times.

Acknowledgements

A great deal of thanks must go to all involved in the design and production of this special edition volume. The following deserve particular mentions: Craig Lamb (design), Dan Sharp (editing), Holly Munro (cover designer) and both Jonathan Schofield and Paul Fincham (reprographics). Their skills, experience and support has been invaluable and each has played a key role in taking my initial idea from its raw elements to this final product.

BRITAIN'S NEW ROYALS

EDITOR:
Jack Harrison
jharrison@mortons.co.uk
PRODUCTION EDITOR:
Dan Sharp
DESIGNER:
Craig Lamb
design_lamb@btinternet.com
COVER DESIGN:
Holly Munro
REPROGRAPHICS:
Paul Fincham and Jonathan Schofield
PUBLISHER:
Steve O'Hara
PUBLISHING DIRECTOR:
Dan Savage
COMMERCIAL DIRECTOR:
Nigel Hole
MARKETING MANAGER:
Charlotte Park
cpark@mortons.co.uk
DISTRIBUTION EXECUTIVE
John Sharratt
tradesales@mortons.co.uk
classicmagazines.co.uk/tradesales

PRINTED BY:
William Gibbons and Sons,
Wolverhampton
ISBN:
978-1-911276-17-3
PUBLISHED BY:

Mortons Media Group Ltd,
Media Centre, Morton Way,
Horncastle, Lincolnshire LN9 6JR.
Tel: 01507 529529
COPYRIGHT:
Mortons Media Group Ltd, 2016
All rights reserved.

Contents

Prince William and the Duchess of Cambridge, future king and queen of Great Britain and the Commonwealth realms and heads of the new generation of British royals. *GF*

The Queen's first grandchildren

Peter Mark Andrew Phillips was the first grandchild of Britain's Queen Elizabeth II and the Duke of Edinburgh, becoming the first member of the new generation of UK royals. At 10.46am on November 15, 1977, he arrived into the world at St Mary's Hospital in the Paddington area of West London and although the nation and its media were interested, the fanfare that would surround later royal births of the 1980s was lacking. There were two main reasons for this: first, although he became the eldest of Her Majesty's grandchildren, he was fifth in line to the throne at the time of his birth and it was not expected he would ever become king; the second was because his parents, Princess Anne and Captain Mark Phillips, did their best to keep their children out of the spotlight.

A little less than three years later on May 15, 1981, Peter gained a sister and the Queen a second grandchild as the royal family welcomed Zara Anne Elizabeth Phillips. Like her brother, Zara was delivered at St Mary's and attracted a comparatively small amount of attention during her early years; Princess Anne and Captain Phillips continuing to shield their children from the limelight with the siblings' main public appearances coming at the annual Trooping the Colour event.

When Princess Anne and Captain Phillips married in 1973 the groom turned down the traditional offer of an earldom, meaning both Peter and Zara are in the unusual position of being grandchildren of a monarch without a royal title, and neither are officially part of the House of Windsor. Perhaps owing to this slight detachment, the two have branched out and have both gone on to forge successful careers in their chosen fields with neither fulfilling any particular set of duties for the monarchy.

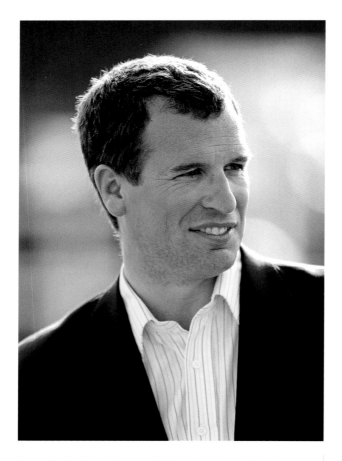

Queen Elizabeth II's eldest grandchild Peter Phillips in 2013. *AM*

The second-eldest grandchild of Her Majesty is Zara Phillips, pictured here in 2014. *JG*

One-year-old Zara Phillips, to the left, joins her brother Peter Phillips for a royal family photo in November 1982. *NP*

The children of Queen Elizabeth II and Prince Philip

Princess Anne, 2014. *ANG*

Princess Anne

BORN:
August 15, 1950
MARRIED:
Captain Mark Phillips,
November 14, 1973
CHILD:
Peter Phillips,
November 15, 1977
CHILD:
Zara Phillips,
May 15, 1981
DIVORCED:
April 23, 1992
MARRIED:
Vice Admiral
Sir Timothy Laurence,
December 12, 1992
CURRENTLY RESIDES:
St James's Palace and
Gatcombe Park

Captain Mark Phillips, 2014. *SP*

Vice Admiral Sir Timothy
Laurence, 2014. *CR*

Princess Anne, in the foreground, smiles as she leaves St Mary's Hospital with her two-day-old son Peter Phillips on November 15, 1977. Carrying Peter is midwife Delphine Stephens who was present at the birth. *PA*

Three-day-old Zara Phillips leaves St Mary's Hospital in the arms of her mother Princess Anne with father Captain Mark Phillips alongside, May 18, 1981. *PA*

Several members of the British royal family – including Queen Elizabeth II, the Duke of Edinburgh, the Queen Mother and Prince Charles – pose for an official portrait to mark the christening of baby Peter Phillips on December 22, 1977. A little more than a month old, Peter is held in the arms of his mother, Princess Anne. *RB*

Peter Phillips with his mother following his christening by the Archbishop of Canterbury in the historic music room at Buckingham Palace, December 22, 1977. *S&G*

Peter Phillips enjoys a ride on his pony Smokey behind Princess Anne at the Sandringham estate with Captain Mark Phillips walking at his side, January 1981. *PA*

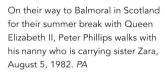

On their way to Balmoral in Scotland for their summer break with Queen Elizabeth II, Peter Phillips walks with his nanny who is carrying sister Zara, August 5, 1982. *PA*

Zara Phillips leaves her nursery school in Gloucestershire on the occasion of her third birthday, May 15, 1984. *PA*

Just days ahead of her fourth birthday, Zara Phillips is carried on the shoulders of Princess Anne at the Royal Windsor Horse Show, May 11, 1985. *PA*

Princess Anne and Peter Phillips at the
Badminton Horse Trials, April 18, 1986. *PA*

After disembarking from the royal yacht *Britannia* at the small Scottish port
of Scrabster in August 1985, the Queen Mother points something out to
members of the royal family including Peter Phillips – standing next to his
great-grandmother – and Zara behind him. *PAN*

Peter and Zara Phillips, along with their pet corgi, brave the rain at
Dauntsey Park in Wiltshire, August 3, 1986. *PA*

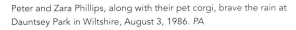

An excited Zara Phillips enjoying her day at the
Minchinhampton Pony Club's summer camp in
Gloucestershire, July 28, 1987. *PA*

A future king is born

At the start of the 1980s Prince Charles was the 31-year-old unmarried heir to the throne of the United Kingdom and questions of who and when he would wed dominated the British press. He was the world's most eligible bachelor at the time and had been linked to a number of glamourous partners. As the decade began it was Lady Diana Spencer who seemed to have stolen his heart.

After six months of dating he proposed marriage during a private dinner at London's Buckingham Palace; Diana accepted immediately. Despite media speculation concerning the pair, they managed to keep the engagement a secret for three weeks before it was officially announced to great excitement across the world.

A congregation of 3500 gathered at St Paul's Cathedral on July 29, 1981, to witness Lady Diana, just 20 years of age, become the Princess of Wales. A further 600,000 filled the streets of the British capital to celebrate and 750 million around the world are estimated to have watched the proceedings on television. After the ceremony the newlyweds travelled back to

Buckingham Palace in an open-topped state carriage before emerging on the balcony of the royal residence for a public kiss. Now married, attention soon turned to when the couple would start a family.

A little less than a year later – on June 21, 1982 – Princess Diana gave birth at St Mary's Hospital and one week later Buckingham Palace announced that the royal family's newest member would be named William Arthur Phillip Louis. Interest in the new prince was huge given that he was now second in line to the throne and had every chance of becoming king of the United Kingdom.

As an heir apparent, and despite the efforts of his parents when he was a child, Prince William has always had to live his life in the spotlight; a life which has included a commitment to traditional royal endeavours such as a military career, charity work and ambassadorial roles. Throughout that time he has enjoyed near constant popularity and, apart from his wife, is perhaps the most adored of Britain's new royals.

Prince Charles and Princess Diana smile and wave to crowds during the procession back to Buckingham Palace following their wedding ceremony. *PA*

Prince William and the Duchess of Cambridge – pictured in New Zealand, 2014 – are at the head of the new generation of UK royals and enjoy huge attention across the world. *AH*

Approaching his second birthday, Prince William plays in the garden of his parents' residence at Kensington Palace, London on June 12, 1984. *PAN*

The children of Queen Elizabeth II and Prince Philip

Prince Charles, 2013. *AM*

Prince Charles

BORN:
November 14, 1948
MARRIED:
Lady Diana Spencer,
becoming Princess Diana,
July 29, 1981
CHILD:
Prince William,
June 21, 1982
CHILD:
Prince Harry,
September 15, 1984
DIVORCED:
August 28, 1996
MARRIED:
Camilla Parker Bowles,
becoming the Duchess of
Cornwall, April 9, 2005
CURRENTLY RESIDES:
Clarence House

Princess Diana, 1997. *JS*

The Duchess of Cornwall,
2013. *DL*

Prince Charles and Princess
Diana introduce their one-day-
old son to the waiting world
outside St Mary's Hospital in
London, June 22, 1982. *TO*

Members of the royal family gathered at Buckingham Palace on August 4, 1982, for the christening of Prince William. Queen Elizabeth II (left) and the Queen Mother (right) sit either side of the future king who is held by his mother Princess Diana. *PA*

Princess Diana shares a playful moment with her baby son Prince William as they prepare for his first Christmas, December 22, 1982... *PA*

... and the newest member of the royal family isn't just doted on by his mother; enjoying time with his father Prince Charles on the same day. *RB*

A two-year-old Prince William enters St Mary's Hospital with Prince Charles, on his way to meet his new baby brother Prince Harry for the first time, September 16, 1984. *PAN*

Prince Charles and Princess Diana held a photocall for Prince William in December 1983, and the young royal didn't disappoint the photographers as he played in the garden at Kensington Palace. *PA*

Now old enough to begin making more regular public appearances, albeit carefully managed, Prince William is accompanied by Red Devils freefall parachute team commander captain Mickey Munn who answered questions for the inquisitive three-year-old during a display by the elite skydivers at Kensington Palace, May 23, 1985. *PAN*

Bridesmaid Laura Fellowes, the niece of Princess Diana, and Prince William at Westminster Abbey for the wedding ceremony of Prince Andrew and the Duchess of York, July 23, 1986. *RB*

Prince William rides in an open coach with Princess Diana and the Queen Mother on June 13, 1987, on their way to the Trooping the Colour ceremony in London. Trooping the Colour is a ceremony performed by regiments of the British and Commonwealth armed forces and has been a tradition of British infantry regiments since the 17th century, although its roots go back much earlier to when a regiment's colours or flags were used as a rallying points on the battlefield. Since 1748, Trooping the Colour has also marked the official birthday of the British monarch and has traditionally been held in London on a Saturday in June. *GA*

Dressed as a motorcycle-mounted British policeman, Prince William plays to the crowd, November 1987. *AH*

Prince William leads his pony out at Highgrove, one his parents' residences in Gloucestershire, December 19, 1987. *PA*

Skiing has long been a favourite pastime for members of the royal family, and Prince William was introduced to the activity at a young age. In April 1991 he's seen leaving the nursery slopes at Lech, Austria, where he was holidaying with Princess Diana and Prince Harry. *MK*

British royals around the world

Princess Beatrice talks to pupils at the Berlin British School in Germany during the first joint overseas engagement that she and her sister Princess Eugenie have embarked upon, January 17, 2013. *TR*

In the Harlem area of New York City, and with a crowd watching on, Prince Harry tests his skills in the batting cages of a baseball training facility, May 14, 2013. *MAT*

Prince William and the Duchess of Cambridge feed a quokka at Taronga Zoo in Sydney, April 21, 2014. AD

British royals around the world

Joined by orphans from the Mants'ase Children's Home, Prince Harry dons his Santa hat during a tour of Maseru, the capital city of Lesotho, December 18, 2014. *CJ*

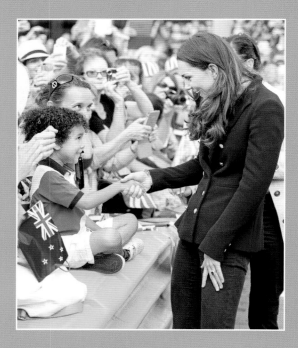

The Duchess of Cambridge meets members of the public at Auckland Harbour during an official tour of New Zealand with her husband on April 11, 2014. *MC*

Prince Harry joins Gonzalo Alvarez to put on a fireman's hat in Valparaíso, Chile, on June 28, 2014. The prince was visiting the city's fire station to meet those who dealt with devastating forest fires which hit the area the previous April. *CJ*

Showing off his culinary skills, Prince William is applauded during a cooking workshop at the Institut de tourisme et d'hôtellerie du Quebec in Montreal, July 2, 2011. *DR*

A tour guide shows Prince Harry around the Colosseum in Rome after he made an unexpected stop at the famous location on the last day of his royal visit to Italy, May 19, 2014. *MD*

On top of their primary focus of charity work and ambassadorial duties, many of Britain's new royals enjoy celebrity status around the world and are cultural icons in their own right. At a basketball match between the Brooklyn Nets and the Cleveland Cavaliers in Brooklyn, New York, on December 8, 2014, Prince William and the Duchess of Cambridge meet Jay Z and Beyoncé as they take their courtside seats. *JB*

British royals around the world

During a nine-day royal tour of the Far East and South Pacific in honour of Queen Elizabeth II's Diamond Jubilee in September, 2012, Prince William and the Duchess of Cambridge dance with locals in Tuvalu, the Solomon Islands. *AE*

Princess Eugenie plays peek-a-boo with a young patient during a visit to the teenage cancer treatment unit at the Hannover Medical School, Germany, January 18, 2013. *CR*

At the Mokolodi Nature Reserve in Botswana, princes William and Harry pose with a rock python, June 15, 2010. *AD*

Prince William and the Duchess of Cambridge attend a jobs fair for veterans and military spouses, held at Sony Pictures Studios in California on July 10, 2011. The prince's own charity does much to support programmes which give assistance to former members of the armed services. *JCH*

Hillary Clinton welcomes the Duchess of Cambridge at a reception in New York in December 2014 to recognise the work of wildlife conservation charity Tusk Trust. The duchess is a patron of the organisation, which is working with the Clinton Foundation and other groups to tackle the issue of wildlife trafficking. *SH*

British royals around the world

Belgian Prime Minister Elio Di Rupo shows Prince William, the Duchess of Cambridge and Prince Harry a book which was signed by King Edward VIII, the uncle of their grandmother Queen Elizabeth II. Britain's new royals were in Belgium for a series of events commemorating the 100th anniversary since the start of the First World War, this particular reception taking place at Mons Town Hall on August 4, 2014. *JB*

The Duchess of Cambridge greets Chinese President Xi Jinping and his wife Peng Liyuan at a creative industry event in London during the pair's official visit to the UK, October 21, 2015. *AH*

During an official visit to the US in December 2014, Prince William and the Duchess of Cambridge visited the National September 11 Memorial & Museum in New York. They toured the landmark which has been built on the site of the former World Trade Center, viewing commemorative installations such as this and leaving flowers by the two reflecting pools. *JB*

At the Inner City Arts Club in Los Angeles, the Duchess of Cambridge checks on the progress of Prince William's work as the pair show off their artistic talents, July 10, 2011. *JS*

Prince Harry is perhaps the most charismatic and outgoing of Britain's new royals. He's pictured in 2014 at the Invictus Games. *CJ*

Princess Beatrice, the fifth grandchild of Queen Elizabeth II, in 2015. *AM*

The only one of Queen Elizabeth II's grandchildren to be born in the 1990s, and the sixth overall, Princess Eugenie, pictured in 2014. *SP*

A new generation grows

Peter Phillips was the first of six new grandchildren for Queen Elizabeth II over the course of 13 years. The fervour surrounding the birth of Prince William had barely settled when Prince Charles and Princess Diana had their second child: Henry Charles Albert David. Prince Harry, as he would soon become known, was born on September 15, 1984, at St Mary's Hospital like his brother and two cousins before him.

While it seemed unlikely that the younger of the siblings would ever be crowned king, interest in the royal baby was still high and the events of the early 1980s – Charles and Diana's wedding and the birth of Prince William – combined with ever increasing news media coverage meant more people were following the day-to-day lives of the royal family than ever before.

The marriage of Queen Elizabeth II's third child – Prince Andrew – on July 23, 1986, only made the spotlight shine more brightly and the press had even more to cover when he and his wife – Sarah Ferguson, now Duchess of York – welcomed Beatrice

Elizabeth Mary, born at the Portland Hospital in London on August 8, 1988. As a male-line grandchild of the ruling monarch, she has the style of Her Royal Highness and the title Princess Beatrice of York.

As was the case for his elder brother and sister, Prince Andrew's second child followed a short time after and on March 23, 1990, the Duchess of York gave birth to another daughter, Eugenie Victoria Helena, once again at the Portland Hospital. Highlighting the intensity of the interest in the young royals, her christening – which took place six months after she was born due to Prince Andrew's commitments in the navy – was the first royal event of its kind to be televised. Like her sister, Beatrice is styled Her Royal Highness and is a Princess of York.

Not yet a year old, Prince Harry is carried by his mother Princess Diana ahead of a trip to the Western Isles. *PA*

The children of Queen Elizabeth II and Prince Philip

Prince Andrew, 2011. *DJ*

Prince Andrew

BORN:
February 19, 1960
MARRIED:
Sarah Ferguson,
becoming the
Duchess of York,
July 23, 1986
CHILD:
Princess Beatrice,
August 8, 1988
CHILD:
Princess Eugenie,
March 23, 1990
CURRENTLY RESIDES:
Buckingham Palace,
The Royal Lodge

The Duchess of York, 2014.
IW

One of the first official photographs released of Prince Andrew and the Duchess of York with their two-week-old daughter Princess Beatrice, August 22, 1988. *PA*

Prince Andrew and the Duchess of York pause outside the Portland Hospital in London holding their new daughter Princess Eugenie, March 1990. *MK*

The royal family attempt to sit for an official photograph at the christening of Prince Harry, held by Princess Diana. Elder brother Prince William has other ideas, December 27, 1984. *AH*

With their father Prince Charles taking part in an all-star charity polo match in aid of British paraplegic sport, princes William and Harry attend an event at Cirencester Park in Gloucestershire, June 6, 1987. *RB*

The Duchess of York and Princess Diana stand behind Princess Beatrice as all three watch a fly-past from the Buckingham Palace balcony following the Trooping the Colour ceremony, June 15, 1991. *MK*

Princesses Beatrice and Eugenie are carried aboard the royal barge at Corpach in Scotland by the Duchess of York on August 12, 1991. The three are on their way to join the royal yacht *Britannia*. *CB*

On the occasion of his sixth birthday, Prince Harry lifts Princess Beatrice on the balcony of Buckingham Palace to see the Battle of Britain 50th anniversary parade taking place in London, September 15, 1990. *MK*

Princess Beatrice sits on the shoulders of the Duchess of York at the Royal Windsor Horse Show, May 11, 1991. *MS*

Not wanting to miss out on the fun, Princess Eugenie enjoys a ride on a slide at the same event three days later. *MS*

Princes William and Harry prepare for a bike ride with their parents around Tresco during their holiday in the Scilly Isles off the coast of Cornwall, June 1, 1989. *PA*

Carrying her skies and poles, Princess Beatrice leaves the chalet in the exclusive Swiss resort of Klosters where she is taking a traditional winter break with her mother and sister, December 30, 1994. *MK*

A young Princess Eugenie gets stuck in the snow as she follows her sister and cousins princes William and Harry to a photocall outside of the hotel in which they are staying during their holiday, January 4, 1995. *MK*

Britain's new royals come together with their extended family at a dinner to mark the diamond wedding anniversary of Queen Elizabeth II and the Duke of Edinburgh on November 18, 2007. Prince William sits on the far left of the front row, with his brother Prince Harry on the far right. Peter Phillips stands on the far left of the third row, with his sister Zara Phillips third from the left on the second row. Princesses Beatrice (left) and Eugenie (right) stand in the centre of the second row either side of their father. The six cousins grew up together in the turbulent 1990s, forming a close bond which still exists today. *TG*

A royal childhood in the 1990s

By the time of the late 1980s and start of the 1990s, the royal family had grown significantly as each of the three eldest of Queen Elizabeth II's children started families of their own. Each of the six parents involved faced an unprecedented situation being under tremendous public and press scrutiny, and the elder family members would have to consider carefully how to guide their young sons and daughters through their formative years in the spotlight.

The simplest and most commonplace activities were given huge coverage: their school life, family holidays, hobbies, sporting interests... none of these seemed to be off limits. Then there were the official engagements and public events that they were expected to attend, at which they had to behave a certain way and demonstrate a maturity far beyond their years.

While they had grown up in high society circles, Princess Diana and the Duchess of York in particular insisted on bringing a sense of normality to their children's lifestyles and undertook such activities as trips to McDonald's and holidays to Disneyland – the sorts of things many children across the UK could relate to. Education was vital too, and the young royals were encouraged to pursue their own interests both in the classroom and in terms of their extracurricular activities. Royal life had its advantages too, and the youngsters were all able to savour moments that most can only dream of.

What's also now apparent is that during this time, the sets of royal siblings and royal cousins formed close bonds during their unique shared experiences, and supported one another as their families faced both intense criticism and terrible tragedy as the decade wore on.

Princes William and Harry enjoying a childhood favourite moment, meeting Father Christmas, backstage during a visit to the International Showjumping Championships in London, December 12, 1990. *MK*

A royal childhood will often mean appearances on the Buckingham Palace balcony for national events. Here, on June 15, 1985, Princess Diana holds Prince Harry with, left to right, Lord Frederick Windsor – son of Prince Michael of Kent – Prince William and Peter Phillips in front of her as they watch the flypast which followed the Trooping the Colour ceremony. *RB*

Churchgoing is an important part of a young royal's life, and here, left to right, Zara Phillips, Prince William and Peter Phillips are seen on the steps of a small church in Sandringham, Norfolk, after 26 members of the royal family attended a Christmas Day service, December 25, 1988. *RB*

Headmistress Frederika Blair-Turner greets Prince William and Princess Diana on the young royal's first day at Wetherby School in Pembridge Square, London, January 15, 1987. *AP*

Peter Phillips follows his sister Zara during a visit to Nailsworth Fire Station in Gloucestershire with their mother Princess Anne, July 16, 1990. *PA*

Photographers followed the young royals across the world in the 1990s, often sparking debate about the extent to which their activities were in the public interest. On April 12, 1990, Princess Diana sits with Prince Harry while Prince William plays in the sand during their holiday in the British Virgin Islands. *EA*

Six-year-old Prince Harry, in the centre, arrives for his school's Christmas carol concert, December 10, 1991. *MK*

There was a great deal of public interest in Prince William in the 1990s and a media frenzy followed his family wherever they went. Excited crowds wanted to meet the future king as well, and he would often greet people at events such as this St David's Day service on March 1, 1991, at Llandaff Cathedral in Cardiff. *MK*

While royal childhood in the 1990s had its pressures, it also had its perks, and Prince William is seen enjoying the action at the British Formula 1 Grand Prix at Silverstone, July 12, 1992. *DJ*

Princess Eugenie, on the left, arrives with the Duchess of York for her first day at Upton House School in Windsor on October 15, 1992. Her sister Princess Beatrice, to the right, has been a pupil there for two years. *TO*

Bridesmaids Princess Beatrice and Princess Eugenie leave the wedding of their former nanny Alison Wardley and royal bodyguard Ben Dady at St Chad church in Withington in Manchester, April 24, 1993. *CRO*

Prince Harry offers a glimpse of his future military career as he dons camouflage gear and rides in a tank during a visit to the barracks of the British Light Dragoons in Hanover, Germany, on July 29, 1993. *MK*

Prince Charles and Prince Harry enjoy a toboggan ride at the Swiss ski resort of Klosters, January 5, 1997. *JS*

Summer breaks at Balmoral, Scotland, have long been a tradition for the British royal family and Prince Charles is pictured with his two sons as they take a morning walk on the banks of the River Dee, August 12, 1997. *CB*

Royal parents have gone to great lengths to ensure their children enjoy similar experiences to other children of the same age. Here Princess Eugenie, right, celebrates her 11th birthday at Disneyland Paris with sister Princess Beatrice and the Duchess of York on May 5, 2001. *PA*

During a formal welcome for members of the royal family at Scrabster in Scotland, Princess Eugenie shows her excitement at seeing her great-grandmother the Queen Mother on August 16, 1997. Princess Beatrice and Prince Andrew follow closely behind. *CB*

On their way to celebrate the Queen Mother's 98th birthday, Queen Elizabeth II is joined by Prince William, Prince Harry, Princess Beatrice and Prince Andrew at Clarence House on August 4, 1998. *JS*

Prince William jokes with Peter Phillips as they board the royal yacht *Britannia* in Portsmouth ahead of their voyage to Balmoral for their traditional summer break on August 7, 1997. The two cousins are close friends, and it's understood that the elder of the two was a pillar of support for the future king in the days and weeks following the death of Princess Diana. *JS*

An important moment in any child's life, Princess Beatrice arrives for her first day at St George's School in Ascot, Berkshire, with her parents Prince Andrew and the Duchess of York, on September 6, 2000. *CI*

British royals and the military

The military careers of both Prince William and Prince Harry have seen them focus much of their subsequent charity work on helping ex-members of the armed forces. On May 20, 2013, they officially opened this Help for Heroes recovery centre in Wiltshire. *BEB*

Appearances and roles at commemorative military events form a large part of the royal duties undertaken by both Prince William and Prince Harry. At a service of remembrance at the Cenotaph in London on November 9, 2014, Prince William prepares to lay a wreath of poppies to remember those who've lost their lives serving in the armed forces. *TI*

Prince Harry on patrol in the deserted town of Garmsir during his time serving in Afghanistan. *JS*

British royals and the military

2008, JS

2008, JS

Prince Harry in Afghanistan

In February 2008, news broke that Prince Harry had been secretly deployed as a forward air controller to Helmand Province in Afghanistan, becoming the first member of the royal family to serve in a war zone since his uncle, Prince Andrew, during the Falklands War.

It was later reported that the prince helped Gurkha troops repel an attack from Taliban insurgents and performed patrol duties in hostile areas, and he was presented with an Operational Service Medal for

Afghanistan by his aunt Princess Anne in May, after he'd returned.

On September 7, 2012, Prince Harry arrived at Camp Bastion to begin a second posting; a four-month combat tour as a co-pilot and gunner for an Apache helicopter. He returned to the UK after 20 weeks in January 2013. This series of images show the prince during his time in Afghanistan in both 2008 and 2012.

2008, JS

2008, JS

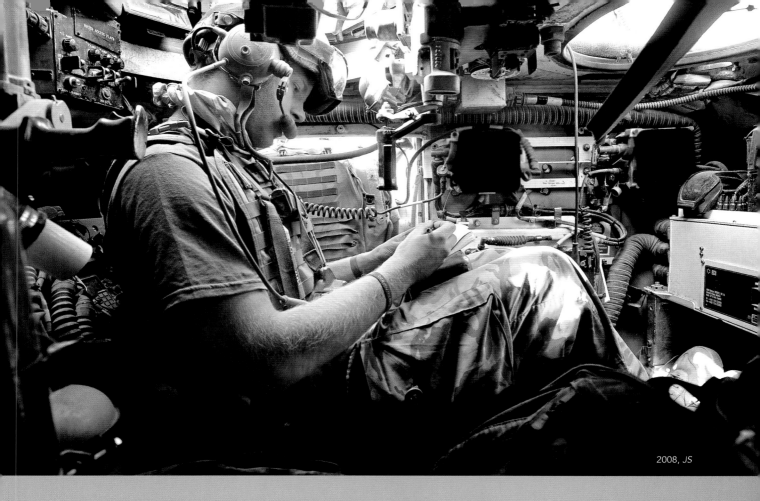

2008, JS

2008, JS

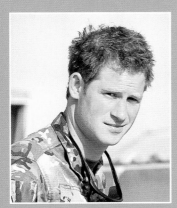

2012, JS

2012, JS

British royals and the military

After being greeted by his brother and father, Prince Harry leaves the departures terminal at RAF Brize Norton following his return from Afghanistan, March 1, 2008. *APA*

Prince William pictured during his Army Officer Selection Board – previously Regular Commissions Board – course in Westbury, as he aims to get accepted to the Royal Military Academy Sandhurst, October 20, 2005. *AH*

At Camp Bastion in Afghanistan, Prince William attends a Remembrance Day service with other British soldiers and political figures, November 14, 2010. *JS*

Graduates of the Royal Military Academy Sandhurst, including Prince William, march at the Sovereign's Parade which is held to mark the passing out of cadets who have completed the institution's Commissioning Course. *BG*

Queen Elizabeth II inspected the line-up on December 15, 2006, and Prince William attempts to suppress a smile as his grandmother walks past. *LW*

As colonel of the regiment, Prince William inspects soldiers of Two Company, 1st Battalion Irish Guards, and presents operational service medals during a parade at Mons Barracks in Aldershot, December 6, 2013. *CC*

British royals and the military

Prince William talks to British veterans of the Korean War following a Korean War Memorial ground-breaking ceremony in central London, November 5, 2013. *RP*

During his annual summer tour of Wales in July 2012, Prince Charles visits RAF Valley on the island of Anglesey to inspect the Sea King search and rescue helicopters based there. His son Prince William was an RAF pilot at the base until September 2013, and the following year he took on a full-time position with the East Anglian Air Ambulance based at Cambridge. The position comes with a salary, but the prince announced he would donate the full amount to the air ambulance charity. *CJ*

Prince Harry interacts with the wheelchair rugby players from Team USA during a medal presentation, May 11, 2016. *CR*

Invictus Games

Created by Prince Harry, the Invictus Games is an international Paralympic-style competition for wounded, injured or sick armed forces men and women during which they go head-to-head in sports such as wheelchair basketball, sitting volleyball and indoor rowing.

The first games was held in 2014 at the Queen Elizabeth Olympic Park in London, with the second event taking place in May 2016 at the ESPN Wide World of Sports at Walt Disney World Resort in Orlando, Florida. It will run again in the Canadian city of Toronto in 2017.

Prince Harry, actor Morgan Freeman and US first lady Michelle Obama listen to speakers during the opening ceremony, May 8, 2016. *JR*

Princess Diana, the mother of princes William and Harry, was a hugely admired and adored member of the royal family even after her marriage with Prince Charles had ended. She found initial popularity as a charming and beautiful young woman and captured hearts during a famous moment in America when she danced with actor John Travolta at a White House reception hosted by President Ronald Reagan and his wife Nancy in November 1985. Later, she would be recognised across the world for her extensive charity work and she's shown, in January 1997, wearing body armour as she tours a minefield in Angola to assess the carnage for herself. 1985, *AH*; 1997, *JS*

The death of Princess Diana

The popularity the royal family enjoyed during the 1980s, brought about by intensive coverage of weddings and births, would come crashing down in the 1990s as a string of controversies rocked the dynasty before the ultimate tragedy brought it to its knees in 1997.

First, in 1992, Prince Andrew and the Duchess of York announced their divorce, swiftly followed by Princess Anne and Captain Mark Phillips. Later that year, a huge fire broke out at the royal residence of Windsor Castle causing significant damage. Queen Elizabeth II called this her "annus horribilis" – Latin for horrible year – in a speech in November, and before it had finished Prince Charles and Princess Diana had separated.

In the months that followed, both revealed intimate details of their marriage breakdown to the press, including the nature of the relationship between the prince and long-term acquaintance Camilla Parker Bowles. It left the reputation of the royal family at a real low, although Princess Diana remained a hugely popular figure for her charity work and the children, being so young, elicited sympathy rather than disdain.

In 1996, final confirmation of the divorce of Prince Charles and Princess Diana seemed to signal an end to a difficult period but on August 31, 1997, the princess was killed as a result of injuries sustained during a car crash in Paris. What followed was an incredible outpouring of public emotion from across the world, matched only by the vilification of Queen Elizabeth II and other senior royals for not issuing a statement, a situation which many viewed as a lack of compassion.

Behind the headlines though, there were two young boys who had lost their mother and Her Majesty said later that shielding them from the hysteria was her primary concern.

The outcry lessened when, on September 5, Queen Elizabeth II spoke to her subjects in a live television address and the next day an estimated three million mourners flocked to London as Princess Diana's funeral took place. An estimated two-and-a-half billion are also believed to have watched on television as princes William and Harry, after much deliberation, bravely followed their mother's coffin during an emotional procession to Westminster Abbey.

The glamorous Princess Diana photographed while attending a dinner at the New York Hilton in December 1995. She was being honoured with a humanitarian award from the United Cerebral Palsy Society. JS

The outpouring of emotion that followed the death of Princess Diana is evidenced by the mass of floral tributes left at the gates of her former home in Kensington Palace on September 2, 1997. *DG*

Once it was announced that singer Elton John would perform a rewritten version of *Candle in the Wind* at Princess Diana's funeral, tributes such as this one in York, pictured on September 4, were seen across the country. *PA*

Candle in the Wind was originally composed by Elton John and Bernie Taupin in 1973 in honour of American actress Marilyn Monroe who had died 11 years earlier. The lyrics were changed for the funeral of Princess Diana and John performed the song – along with piano solo – during the service. In the weeks after it reached number one in the charts of many countries and went on to become the second biggest-selling single of all time behind Bing Crosby's *White Christmas*. *PA*

A policeman throws a bunch of flowers on to The Mall as Princess Diana's coffin is taken from Westminster Abbey to her final resting place of Althorp where a private burial was to take place later the same day, September 6, 1997. JOG

In what has become one of the most iconic royal photographs ever, princes William and Harry – either side of Princess Diana's brother Earl Spencer – walk behind their mother's coffin as it makes its way to Westminster Abbey for her funeral on September 6, 1997. On either end of the line are the Duke of Edinburgh, left, who insisted on supporting his young grandsons, and Prince Charles, right, the former husband of the princess. AB

The funeral cortege of Princess Diana arrives at Westminster Abbey, September 6, 1997. PA

New royals in the new millennium

Press and public obsession with the affairs of the royal family peaked with the death of Princess Diana and the fevered speculation that had surrounded it subsided as a new millennium beckoned.

The royal family, with Queen Elizabeth II at its head, accepted that it had to modernise in the wake of what had happened and so to reclaim its standing worldwide it embarked upon a more professional public relations campaign. At the centre of this were Britain's newest royals who were now young adults.

Taking on a more outward facing role and making far more appearances, the cousins were far better placed to connect with British youth than their parents or grandparents and took to the task with ease. With princes William and Harry at the forefront, the youngsters also embarked on several charitable activities, carrying on the legacy of Princess Diana.

During this time, two more grandchildren were born to Queen Elizabeth II, taking the number of Britain's new royals to eight.

In June, 1999, Her Majesty's youngest son Prince Edward had married Sophie Rhys-Jones, who became the Countess of Wessex, and shortly after – on November 8, 2003 – they welcomed Louise Alice Elizabeth Mary who was delivered by Caesarean section at Frimley Park Hospital in Surrey. Four years later and Lady Louise Windsor – her official title – had a brother, James Alexander Phillip Theo who holds the title James, Viscount Severn.

While the youngest members of this generation of royals were growing up, the older members had come of age and on May 17, 2008, Peter Phillips married Canadian Autumn Kelly at Windsor Castle. His sister Zara Phillips announced her own engagement to England World Cup-winning rugby international Mike Tindall in 2010. It was the future of Prince William that generated most interest, however, and in the late 2000s speculation mounted that he himself might soon get down on one knee and propose marriage to his rumoured long-term girlfriend Catherine Middleton whom he met while at university.

Britain's two young princes have become hugely popular figures across the globe, in part due to the charity work they undertake which has been inspired by their mother, Princess Diana. On the left, Prince Harry congratulates Prince William after running in the fund-raising Sport Relief Mile in 2004, while on the right the duo are seen in 2005 packing relief items bound for the Maldives. 2004, *CY*; 2005, *BB*

Prince William and Prince Harry don suits and bowler hats for an armed forces event at London's Hyde Park in May 2007. Despite the pressures of royal life, the pair have excelled at connecting with and reflecting young people in the UK and the world as part of a reinvigorated PR effort by the British monarchy. *SR*

The children of Queen Elizabeth II and Prince Philip

Prince Edward, 2014. *JS*

Prince Edward

BORN:
March 10, 1964
MARRIED:
Sophie Rhys-Jones,
becoming the
Countess of Wessex,
June 19, 1999
CHILD:
Lady Louise Windsor,
November 8, 2003
CHILD:
James, Viscount Severn,
December 17, 2008
CURRENTLY RESIDES:
Buckingham Palace,
Bagshot Park

The Countess of Wessex,
2015. *JB*

Prince Edward and the Countess of Wessex leave Frimley Park Hospital in Surrey with their newborn baby daughter Lady Louise Windsor, November 23, 2003. *JGG*

Prince William teaches an English lesson to Chilean schoolchildren aged 10 and 11 at a school in the village of Tortel on December 7, 2000. He was in the country during his expedition with international volunteer organisation Raleigh International where he lived with other young teachers, shared household chores and hosted a show on the local radio station. *TM*

Three-day-old James, Viscount Severn is taken home from Frimley Park Hospital by his parents Prince Edward and the Countess of Wessex, December 20, 2007. *DP*

A member of the public hands Prince William a birthday balloon on June 19, 2003, as he leaves the Newport Action for the Single Homeless charity building in South Wales. Accompanied by Prince Charles, the visit is one of several arranged across the UK to mark the future king turning 21 two days later. *CI*

Celebrating the Duke of Edinburgh's 80th birthday, Prince Harry arrives at St George's Chapel in Windsor for a service of thanksgiving with, left to right, Princess Eugenie, Princess Xenia of Saxony and Princess Beatrice, June 10, 2001. *FH*

At the Guards Polo Club in Windsor, Prince Harry takes in some refreshments following the Golden Jubilee Trophy game, July 30, 2006. APA

Peter Phillips and Autumn Kelly share a joke with England international rugby player Mike Tindall as they arrive for a day at the horse races in Cheltenham, March 16, 2006. BB

After gaining an upper second class honours degree in geography, Prince William meets crowds following his graduation ceremony from the University of St Andrews in Scotland, June 23, 2005. DC

Prince Harry spent part of his gap year between school and university in Australia, taking part in activities such as herding bulls on his horse Guardsman, November 2003. GC

Zara Phillips at the Red Cross Ball in south London's Room by the River, November 21, 2007. *SM*

During a visit to the Winnicott Baby Unit at St Mary's – the hospital where he himself was born – Prince William holds newborn Sina Nuru as he is shown around the new facility, September 20, 2006. *TH*

Following their wedding ceremony, Peter and Autumn Phillips leave Windsor's St George's Chapel, May 17, 2008. *SC*

Sisters and princesses Beatrice and Eugenie arrive by horse-drawn carriage at the first day of the Royal Ascot horse races meeting in Berkshire, June 17, 2008. *AH*

Princesses Beatrice and Eugenie pose for a photograph at the residence of the British ambassador in Germany, 2013. *CJ*

Britain's new royals

Prince William, the Duchess of Cambridge and Prince Harry during an event at the Imperial War Museum in London, 2011. *AE*

The Duchess of Cambridge pushes Princess Charlotte in her pram following her christening, while Prince George is carried by his father, 2015. *MT*

Prince William shows his grandmother Queen Elizabeth II around RAF Valley in Anglesey where he was stationed during his time as an RAF search and rescue pilot, 2011. CF

Prince William and the Duchess of
Cambridge take in the scenery
after their trek to the Paro
Taktsang – or Tiger's Nest –
monastery near Paro in Bhutan,
which they visited as part of their
six-day royal tour of the region,
April 15, 2016. JG

Britain's new royals

Prince William and the Duchess of Cambridge visit the Taj Mahal in India during a seven-day visit royal visit to India and Bhutan, 2016. *DLP*

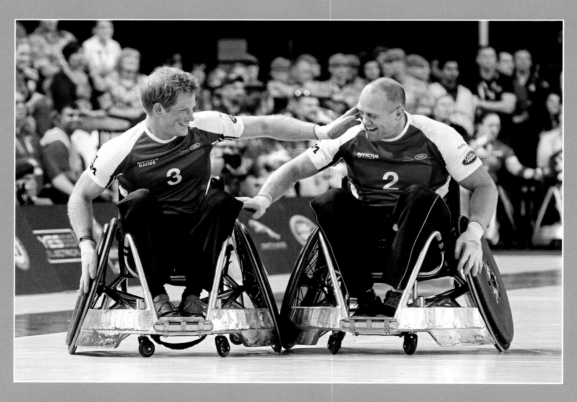

Prince Harry tackles Mike Tindall as they take part in a wheelchair rugby exhibition match in London, 2014. *YM*

Zara Phillips jokes with
Prince Harry outside
St George's Chapel at
Windsor following the
wedding of Peter
Phillips and Autumn
Phillips, 2008. *AH*

Britain's new royals

The royal family watch a flypast from the balcony of Buckingham Palace during the annual Trooping the Colour parade, 2012. *DLP*

Prince Harry, the Duchess of Cambridge and Prince William attend the Service of Commemoration at St Paul's Cathedral which was held to mark the end of British combat operations in Afghanistan, 2015. *AH*

Prince William and the Duchess of Cambridge depart the Metropolitan Museum of Art in New York, 2014. *JM*

Britain's new royals

The Duchess of Cambridge, Prince William and Prince Harry take a tour of the 'Blood Swept Lands and Seas of Red' poppy installation at the Tower of London, 2014. *MAD*

The young royals watch riders during the Tour de France which commenced in Britain in 2014. *CJ*

Princess Charlotte makes her first appearance on the balcony of Buckingham Palace for the Trooping the Colour flypast, joined by the Duchess of Cambridge, Prince William, Prince George and Prince Harry, 2016. *DLP*

The Duchess of Cambridge and Prince William watch track cycling at the velodrome during the summer Olympic Games in London, August 2, 2012. *MR*

Prince William and Kate Middleton,
the Duke and Duchess of Cambridge

Speculation was rife in 2003 that Britain's future king was dating and that the lucky lady's name was Catherine Middleton, known simply as Kate. The pair, who first met in 2001, had been flatmates at the University of St Andrews and when Miss Middleton attended Prince William's passing out parade at Royal Sandhurst Military Academy, British bookmakers began taking bets on the chances of an imminent royal wedding.

Media attention became so intense that they reportedly split for a short period, Prince William going so far as to ask the paparazzi to keep their distance from his rumoured girlfriend. Miss Middleton continued to appear at events with the young royal, however, including the Concert for Diana on July 1, 2007, which was organised by princes William and Harry in honour of their mother.

Three years later came the news the world had been waiting for: Prince William was to marry. On November 16, 2010, Clarence House announced that he had proposed to Miss Middleton while the two were in Kenya and a wedding date of July 29, 2011, was set. The event was a public holiday in the UK and attracted more than a million well-wishers to London who lined the route that the couple would take from the ceremony

at Westminster Abbey back to Buckingham Palace. The global television audience was estimated to be in excess of 300 million, viewing figures in Great Britain alone peaked at a staggering 37 million, and there were a number of tributes from people and governments across the Commonwealth and throughout the world.

After the ceremony and the open carriage ride back to Buckingham Palace, Prince William and the new Duchess of Cambridge delighted the watching crowds by appearing on the balcony of the royal residence before the groom drove his new wife a short distance up The Mall back to Clarence House in a two-seater Aston Martin DB6. The destination of their honeymoon was a closely guarded secret and despite reports that the couple would leave immediately, Prince William returned to his job as a search-and-rescue pilot before they eventually departed for the Seychelles on May 9, some 10 days after the wedding.

On the morning of May 21, it was announced that the newlyweds had returned to the UK, Prince William was back at work and the Duchess of Cambridge was preparing for their first overseas tour as a married couple to Canada and the US which began on June 30.

It's all smiles for Kate Middleton as she arrives at the Renaissance Rooms in London for the Day-Glo Midnight Roller Disco on September 20, 2008. Miss Middleton had organised the event in memory of her friend Thomas Waley-Cohen who died from bone cancer in 2004 aged just 20. *JGG*

Kate Middleton in good spirits as she hosts Time to Reflect, an exhibition of limited edition photographs of celebrities, in order to raise funds for UNICEF, November 29, 2007. *FH*

A photograph of Bucklebury, a small village in Berkshire, taken in January 2011. This is the location of the Duchess of Cambridge's family home. *SP*

CHAPTER 8

One of the most talked about couples in the world; Kate Middleton and Prince William leave the wedding of their friends Harry Mead and Rosie Bradford in Gloucestershire on October 23, 2010. *CI*

Kate Middleton and Prince William pose during a photocall at St James's Palace following the announcement of their engagement, November 16, 2010. *JS*

Now the fiancée of Prince William, Kate Middleton meets members of the public during a Royal National Lifeboat Institution event in Wales, February 24, 2011. *PN*

Just days ahead of their wedding, Prince William and Kate Middleton visit Witton Country Park in Lancashire to see outdoor activities taking place as part of the Queen Elizabeth II Fields Challenge, April 11, 2011. *APR*

As crowds gather outside the Goring Hotel in London, Kate Middleton waves as she prepares to spend her last night as a single woman at the venue before marrying Prince William the following day, April 28, 2011. *JR*

Kate Middleton flips a pancake with six-year-old Ellie Tang at a display by the Northern Ireland Cancer Fund for Children outside Belfast City Hall, March 8, 2011. *NC*

Prince William and Kate Middleton
The royal wedding, April 29, 2011

Kate Middleton arrives at Westminster Abbey ahead of her wedding ceremony. *GF*

Best man Prince Harry and maid of honour Pippa Middleton. *CM*

The royal couple exchange their vows. *DT*

Prince William jokes
with his best man
Prince Harry. *ANM*

Prince William and Kate Middleton
The royal wedding, April 29, 2011

Michael Middleton gives his daughter away at the altar. *DLP*

Princess Eugenie, left, and Princess Beatrice, right, make their way in to Westminster Abbey. *SP*

Zara Phillips and her fiancé Mike Tindall leave the wedding reception which took place at Buckingham Palace. *JS*

Here comes the bride… Kate Middleton is walked down the aisle by her father Michael, followed by her sister and maid of honour Pippa. *ANM*

Prince William and Kate Middleton
The royal wedding, April 29, 2011

The bride and groom exchange rings in front of the Archbishop of Canterbury. *ANM*

Husband and wife Prince William and the Duchess of Cambridge depart Westminster Abbey to make their way to Buckingham Palace. *SR*

The newlyweds give the crowds what they want to see by appearing on the Buckingham Palace balcony for a kiss. *JS*

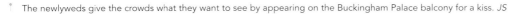

Prince William and Kate Middleton
The royal wedding, April 29, 2011

The view looking down The Mall from Buckingham Palace as a huge crowd waits to see the happy couple appear on the balcony. *RN*

Well-wishers get what they've been waiting for as Prince William and the Duchess of Cambridge emerge with the royal family as the Battle of Britain Memorial Flight roars overhead. *CI*

The groom drives himself and his new wife as they leave the Buckingham Palace reception for Clarence House. *CI*

Prince William and the Duchess of Cambridge walk hand-in-hand from Buckingham Palace on the day after their wedding. *JS*

As part of their official royal tour of Canada, Prince William and the Duchess of Cambridge are greeted by a large crowd as they arrive in the province of Prince Edward Island, July 4, 2011. *IV*

The royal couple attend the UK Trade & Investment reception at the Beverley Hilton Hotel in California on July 8, 2011. *LH*

Prince William and the Duchess of Cambridge wear traditional clothes during a visit to the home of Governor General Frank Kabui in the Solomon Islands which is part of a nine-day royal tour, September 16, 2012. *CJ*

The news that the Duchess of Cambridge was expecting a baby had to be revealed after the mother-to-be was admitted to hospital suffering acute morning sickness in December 2012. Prince William accompanies his wife after she's been discharged. *AH*

Prince William sits on the Batpod from the Batman series of films during a visit to the Warner Bros. studios in Hertfordshire on April 26, 2013. The Duchess of Cambridge, six months pregnant, clearly sees the funny side. *CJ*

At London's Natural History Museum, Prince William and the Duchess of Cambridge wear 3D glasses prior to a screening of David Attenborough's Natural History Museum Alive film, December 11, 2013. *SUP*

Followed by Peter Phillips, Mike Tindall and, in the background, Prince Edward, the Duchess of Cambridge and Prince William arrive at St Mary Magdalene Church on the Sandringham royal estate for the traditional Christmas Day service, December 25, 2013. *JG*

Prince William and the Duchess of Cambridge visit the Valero Pembroke Refinery in Wales, November 8, 2014. *AH*

The Duchess of Cambridge shows off her cricket skills as she joins former Indian captain Dilip Vengsarkar for a game in Mumbai, April 10, 2016. *RM*

At London's Royal Albert Hall, Prince William and the Duchess of Cambridge attend the annual Royal British Legion Festival of Remembrance which commemorates and honours all those who have lost their lives in conflicts, November 7, 2015. *CJ*

Prince Harry, the Duchess of Cambridge and Prince William visit the Royal Horticultural Society Chelsea Flower Show, May 23, 2016. *ALP*

The Duchess of Cambridge:
Style icon

Kate Middleton, the Duchess of Cambridge, is one of the most stylish women in the world and has had a major impact upon fashion in both the United Kingdom and America. Whether it's her high-end designer wardrobe, high street brands or recycled outfits, wherever she appears there is interest and the duchess has featured in and topped several of the most prominent 'best dressed' lists since she came onto the public scene in the mid-2000s. The 'Kate Middleton Effect', as it's become known, is a trend whereby clothes or fashion accessories that she is seen wearing experience rapid increases in sales and are often unavailable shortly thereafter. If evidence was needed of her status as a fashion icon, it came in June 2016 when the duchess took part in a shoot for *Vogue's* centenary issue, appearing on the cover of the famous magazine.

The centenary issue of *Vogue* magazine which featured the Duchess of Cambridge on its cover, May 5, 2016. *IW*

2011, DC

2012, LSS

2015, CJ

2015, GF

British royals outside royal life

Zara Phillips holds her BBC Sports Personality of the Year trophy, which she won in 2006. She was given the award, which is voted for by the British public, after winning both the world and European equestrian titles that year on her horse Toytown. *CR*

Spending a day at the races has long been a favourite pastime of the British royal family, and princesses Beatrice and Eugenie enjoy the action on Derby Day at Epsom racecourse in Surrey, June 1, 2013. *DLP*

The Duchess of Cambridge, Prince William and Prince Harry pose for a photo with children at the Commonwealth Games village in Glasgow, July 29, 2014. *DL*

Great Britain's Zara Tindall celebrates after receiving her silver medal on day four of the Olympic Games in London, July 31, 2012.
ANM

British royals outside royal life

Prince Harry, Prince William and the Duchess of Cambridge watch the England v Italy match at Twickenham during the annual Six Nations rugby tournament, February 10, 2007. AG

Britain's young royals threw their support behind the 2012 Olympic Games in London, and Princess Beatrice holds her finisher's medal after a completing a five-mile run around the Olympic Park where that summer's event would take place, March 31, 2012. MAC

Education has been an important part of life for Britain's young royals and Princess Eugenie smiles proudly on July 11, 2012, after her graduation ceremony from Newcastle University. July 11, 2012. OH

Demonstrating their enjoyment of books and movies, Prince Harry, the Duchess of Cambridge and Prince William excitedly wave their wands in Diagon Alley during a visit to the set of Harry Potter at Warner Bros. studios in Hertfordshire, April 26, 2013. *PR*

Jamaican sprinter Usain Bolt teaches his signature pose to Prince Harry after a short race at the University of the West Indies on March 6, 2012. *JS*

British royals outside royal life

Cheering Team GB cyclist Chris Hoy across the line to his sixth Olympic gold medal are Prince Harry and Peter Phillips, with former Prime Minister John Major in front, August 7, 2012. *JS*

Both Prince William and Prince Harry are avid motorcyclists, and the elder brother paid a visit to Motorcycle Live at Birmingham's NEC on November 30, 2013. During his walk around the event, he posed for pictures while sitting on a Triumph. *JG*

Prince William enjoys a kickabout during the first ever football match to be hosted within the grounds of Buckingham Palace on October 7, 2013. The contest, which was the prince's idea, was hosted to mark the 150th anniversary of the English Football Association and saw two of the first teams ever to be formed in England to head-to-head. The result was a 2-1 win for Polytechnic FC, set up in 1875, against Civil Service FC which was created in 1863. Before the game, Prince William told players that if anyone broke a window, they would have to "answer to the Queen". *JS*

At the Inspire Suffolk centre for young people, Prince Harry prepares to save a penalty, May 29, 2014. *JS*

At the Tollcross International Swimming Centre in Glasgow, Prince William and the Duchess of Cambridge watch the action at the Commonwealth Games, July 28, 2014. *ANM*

British royals outside royal life

Princess Beatrice works the phones on the trading floor during the BGC Charity Day in London on September 11, 2014. The event is held annually by BGC Partners and Cantor Fitzgerald to commemorate 658 employees who perished on September 11, 2001, during the terrorist attacks in New York. One hundred per cent of global revenues on Charity Day are distributed to organisations worldwide. Since its inception, it has raised about $125 million. *IW*

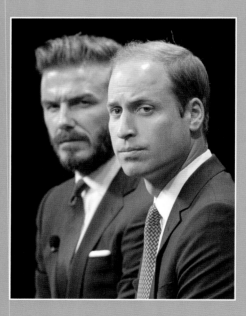

Prince William plays in a charity polo match at Cirencester Park Polo Club, June 15, 2014. *AH*

Sports and animal welfare have been two of Prince William's key interests, and the two crossed over on June 9, 2014, at a United for Wildlife campaign which aims to harness the power of sport to raise awareness of conservation issues around the world. He is pictured during the event at Google Town Hall in London with former England international footballer David Beckham. *AH*

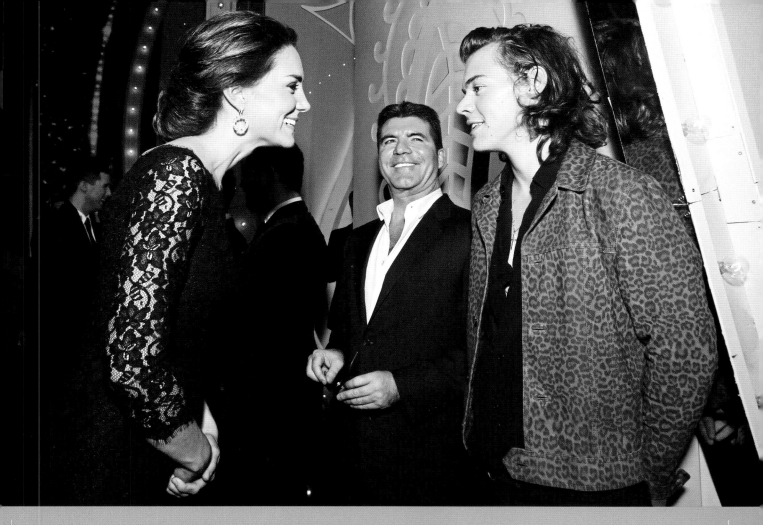

One Direction's Harry Styles talks to the Duchess of Cambridge at the Royal Variety Performance in London, with Simon Cowell watching, on November 13, 2014. *YM*

On February 17, 2016, the Duchess of Cambridge became guest editor of news website *The Huffington Post* for the day. She's pictured talking to news editor James Martin, seated, and editor-in-chief Stephen Hull in a temporary newsroom set up at Kensington Palace. *CJ*

Mike and Zara Tindall emerge from Edinburgh's Canongate Kirk as husband and wife following their wedding ceremony on July 30, 2011. *DM*

Births and marriages, marriages and births

I n the late 2000s and early 2010s the world was captivated by the courtship and marriage of Prince William and the Duchess of Cambridge, but the royal family was growing in other ways too. On December 29, 2010, Peter and Autumn Phillips gave Queen Elizabeth II her first great-grandchild when they welcomed a daughter, Savannah Anne Kathleen Phillips, at Gloucestershire Royal Hospital.

The royal weddings came thick and fast also, and just three months after Prince William and the Duchess of Cambridge had tied the knot Zara Phillips became Zara Tindall as she wed fiancé Mike at the Canongate Kirk in Edinburgh, Scotland, on July 30, 2011.

Additions to the royal family, whether by marriage or birth, continued apace as the 2010s progressed and on March 29, 2012, Peter and Autumn Phillips had a second daughter – Isla Elizabeth. As it stands, the two children are 14th and 15th in line to the throne. Later that year came the news the world had been waiting for when, on December 3, 2012, it was announced that Prince William and the Duchess of Cambridge were expecting their first child. Huge excitement swept the UK and overseas in anticipation of the birth of a future king or queen and when the Duchess was admitted to St Mary's Hospital in London in the early stages of labour on July 22, 2013, the world's media descended on the British capital.

Savannah Phillips, right, and her sister Isla, left, have fun on a bouncy slide with family friend Megan McCarthy during the Festival of British Evening at Gatcombe Park, Gloucestershire, August 3, 2014. *AH*

Resplendent bride Zara Phillips arrives at Canongate Kirk in Edinburgh for her wedding to Mike Tindall, July 30, 2011. *DM*

Autumn Phillips with her seven-month-old daughter Savannah at Gatcombe Park's Festival of British Eventing, August 6, 2011. *TI*

The eldest of Queen Elizabeth II's great-grandchildren Savannah Phillips enjoys a spring day out, March 24, 2012. *AH*

At the Beaufort Polo Club where princes William and Harry are playing in a charity match, the Duchess of Cambridge lets Savannah Phillips take the lead of her dog Lupo, June 17, 2012. *AH*

Riding the carousel at the Royal Windsor Horse Show are Peter and Autumn Phillips, along with their two children Savannah and Isla, May 17, 2014. SP

At the same event the following year on May 16, Savannah and Isla walk with their parents at the equine event held at Windsor Castle. SP

Shortly after her first birthday, Isla Phillips enjoys a snack while watching the Badminton Horse Trials with her mother Autumn, May 4, 2013. AH

Town crier Tony Appleton announces the birth of Prince George outside St Mary's Hospital, Monday, July 22, 2013. *LP*

Prince George of Cambridge

The Duchess of Cambridge gave birth to a baby boy weighing eight pounds and six ounces on July 22, 2013. The occasion was a momentous one: Prince William and the Duchess had their first child, a future king had been born and for only the second time in the history three generations of direct heirs to the British throne were alive.

A traditional bulletin announcing the royal arrival was displayed on an easel outside Buckingham Palace, but in a break with usual protocol the royal residence had first issued a press release to disclose the news. Gun salutes marked the birth in the capitals of several Commonwealth nations, including London, and the bells of Westminster Abbey and other churches were rung in celebration.

Prince William, the Duchess of Cambridge and their son left hospital on July 23, and the following day the newborn baby's name was revealed as George Alexander Louis.

Like Princess Diana before her, the Duchess of Cambridge has endeavoured to keep her young son away from the glaring lenses of the media.

Despite making an official visit to Australia with his parents in April 2014, when Prince George revisited the hospital of his birth to meet his new sister –Charlotte Elizabeth Diana born on May 2, 2015 – it was just his second public appearance.

While it did not reach the same heights as the news of her brother's birth, there was considerable fanfare to mark the arrival of Princess Charlotte and many famous landmarks such as Tower Bridge, the London Eye and the fountain at Trafalgar Square were illuminated pink.

Before he'd gained a sister, Prince George also had a new cousin when on January 17, 2014, Mike and Zara Tindall had their first child, Mia Grace.

Prince William and Prince George arrive at St Mary's Hospital to visit the Duchess of Cambridge following the birth of Princess Charlotte on May 2, 2015. This was just the second public appearance for the young royal, his first being nearly two years earlier when he was brought out of hospital by his parents. AG

Two contrasting images from outside the Lindo Wing of St Mary's Hospital in central London: above, the world's media gathers in the press pen on July 15, 2013, as the Duchess of Cambridge approaches her due date; then below, as she, Prince William and Prince George emerge for the first time. The cameras take images which will be beamed across the globe. Above, *YM*; Below *DL*

Prince William arrives with Prince George for the newborn royal's christening by Archbishop of Canterbury Justin Welby at the Chapel Royal in St James's Palace on October 23, 2013. *JS*

The baby is then carried out by the Duchess of Cambridge following the service. *JS*

Prince William, the Duchess of Cambridge and Prince George visit Plunket, a child welfare group, at Government House in Wellington, New Zealand, April 9, 2014. *PA*

Prince George and the Duchess of Cambridge, along with Prince William, arrive at the Military Terminal in Wellington International Airport to start their official tour of New Zealand and later Australia, April 7, 2014. *AD*

During their three-week tour of Australia and New Zealand, Prince William and Prince George look at the animals in Taronga Zoo in Sydney, April 20, 2014. *CJ*

Appearing on the Buckingham Palace balcony for the flypast during the Trooping the Colour ceremony is a rite of passage for any young royal, and Prince George gets his first taste in the arms of Prince William on June 13, 2015. Joining the pair, from left to right, are the Duchess of Cornwall, Prince Charles, Queen Elizabeth II, the Duchess of Cambridge, Prince Harry and James, Viscount Severn. *JB*

Princess Charlotte of Cambridge is born. Prince William and the Duchess of Cambridge present their newborn daughter to the world outside St Mary's Hospital, London, May 2, 2015. *DLO*

Princess Charlotte is the star of the show at her christening, getting plenty of attention from her great-grandparents Queen Elizabeth II and the Duke of Edinburgh, left, and the Duchess of Cornwall, in the centre. *CJ*

And pushed in her Silver Cross pram, the baby heads to the church of St Mary Magdalene in Sandringham, Norfolk, to be christened by Archbishop of Canterbury Justin Welby, July 5, 2015. *CJ*

Mike Tindall celebrates with his wife Zara and daughter Mia after completing a quadrathlon sporting challenge in Scotland, July 11, 2015. *AM*

Prince William and the Duchess of Cambridge, with their children Prince George and Princess Charlotte, enjoy a short skiing break in the French Alps, March 7, 2016. *JS*

Savannah Phillips holds the hand of her cousin Mia Tindall as they walk with Isla Phillips to watch Zara Tindall complete in a showjumping competition during the fifth day of the Badminton Horse Trials, May 8, 2016. *SP*

US President Barack Obama talks with Prince William during a visit to the UK in April 2016, as two-and-a-half year old Prince George plays on a rocking horse bought for him by the American leader shortly after his birth. Sales of the robe worn by Prince George rocketed after the image was released, an example of the Prince George Effect – the trend that sees any product or item of clothing used by the young royal shoot up in popularity. Such is his influence, that *GQ* magazine has ranked him as number 49 on its list of the 50 best-dressed men in Britain. In the foreground of this image, First Lady Michelle Obama and Prince Harry are deep in discussion, perhaps about the Invictus Games – a sporting event for wounded, injured and sick servicemen and women founded by the prince and keenly supported by Mrs Obama. *PS-WH* *

Prince William, Prince Harry, the Duchess of Cambridge and Peter Phillips at The Mall during the Patron's Lunch in London, part of the Queen at 90 celebrations, June 12, 2016. *AE*

The Queen at 90

Throughout 2016, Britain's new royals have been at the centre of celebrations to mark the historic 90th birthday of Queen Elizabeth II. Prince William has joined his grandmother at several of the landmark occasions to have taken place, including giving her an introduction at the public lunch party held in her honour in London in June. This active role demonstrates the prince's enduring popularity and ever-increasing level of responsibility within the monarchy.

Peter Phillips, not usually a public-facing member of the royal family, has also been heavily involved and headed up the organisation of the event which took place on The Mall leading up to Buckingham Palace. All other prominent members of the royal family appeared, either in London or at other celebrations across the UK, showing support for their grandmother and meeting the public during several walkabouts which Queen Elizabeth II and her mother made famous.

It's been a busy year away from the fanfare of the royal birthday too, as the new generation of British royals embark upon even more high-profile engagements and activities under the watchful eye of the world's media. For Prince Harry, the focus of 2016 has been on the Invictus Games – a sporting event he devised for wounded and sick armed forces personnel across the world. The Duchess of Cambridge meanwhile hit the headlines, in more ways than one, when she guest edited *The Huffington Post* news website to raise awareness of issues surrounding mental health.

While Her Majesty remains a fully active head of state and has consistently reaffirmed her commitment to her role, as she enters her 91st year there can be little doubt that her schedule will be scaled back. For Britain's new royals this will mean more responsibility as they play central roles in the leadership of the UK and Commonwealth whether it is their official royal duties, ambassadorial roles, professional positions, personal interests or charitable pursuits.

Zara Tindall on horseback during a televised event at Windsor Castle held to celebrate the 90th birthday of Queen Elizabeth II, May 15, 2016. *AM*

Princess Eugenie, left, and Princess Beatrice, right, arrive at St Paul's Cathedral for a national service of thanksgiving in honour of Her Majesty, June 10, 2016. *SR*

Prince William delivers a speech on The Mall to introduce Queen Elizabeth II at her 90th birthday picnic lunch, June 12, 2016. *AE*

Prince Harry stops for pictures with well-wishers on The Mall at Queen Elizabeth II's birthday lunch, June 12, 2016. *AE*

From left to right, Prince Andrew, Princess Beatrice, Princess Eugenie, Princess Anne, Sir Timothy Laurence, Peter Phillips, Autumn Phillips, Zara Tindall and Mike Tindall attend the service of thanksgiving for Queen Elizabeth II at St Paul's Cathedral, June 10, 2016. *IV*

Princess Eugenie, left, and Princess Beatrice, right, arrive in a carriage during the Trooping the Colour ceremony in central London, June 11, 2016. *JS*

Prince Harry joins the Duchess of Cornwall and the Duchess of Cambridge in a carriage as the royal procession makes its way from Buckingham Palace to Horse Guards Parade for the Trooping the Colour ceremony, June 11, 2016. *YM*

Prince George and Princess Charlotte join senior members of the royal family on the Buckingham Palace balcony, part of a series of events marking the 90th birthday of Queen Elizabeth II. *YM*

From the Press Association archive, a nine-year-old Prince William joins his brother Prince Harry, aged seven, as they board the royal yacht *Britannia* on the Toronto waterfront in Canada, October 23, 1991. *MK*

PRESS ASSOCIATION IMAGES, PAIMAGES.CO.UK

Unless otherwise stated, the images in this edition are courtesy of the Press Association.

IMAGE COLLECTIONS:

AP/Press Association Images; Daily Mail/PA Archive/Press Association Images; Daily Mail/PA Wire/Press Association Images; Daily Mirror/PA Archive/Press Association Images; EMPICS Entertainment; Evening Standard/NPA/PA Archive/Press Association Images; PA Archive/Press Association Images; PA Wire/Press Association Images; S&G Barratts/EMPICS Archive; The Daily Telegraph/PA Archive/Press Association Images; The Daily Telegraph/PA Wire/Press Association Images; The Sun/PA Archive/Press Association Images; The Sun/PA Wire/Press Association Images; The Telegraph/PA Wire/Press Association Images; The Times/PA Archive/Press Association Images

INDIVIDUAL PHOTOGRAPHERS:

Adam Butler (AB); Alastair Grant (AG); Alpha Press (ALP); Andrew Matthews (AM); Andrew Milligan (ANM); Andrew Parsons (APA); Anna Gowthorpe (ANG); Anthony Devlin (AD); Anwar Hussein (AH); Arrow Press (APR); Arthur Edwards (AE); Associated Press (AP); Barry Batchelor (BB); Ben Birchall (BEB); Ben Gurr (BG); Bruce Adams (BA); Carl Court (CC); Cavan Pawson (CPA); Chris Bacon (CB); Chris Ison (CI); Chris Jackson (CJ); Chris Radburn (CR); Chris Young (CY); Christopher Furlong (CF); Christopher Pledger (CP); Clara Molden (CM); Croft (CRO); Daniel Leal-Olivas (DLO); Danny Lawson (DL); Dave Thompson (DT); David Cheskin (DC); David Giles (DG); David Jones (DJ); David Parry (DP); David Rose (DR); Dominic Lipinski (DLP); Dylan Martinez (DM); Eddie Mulholland (EM); Elsie Amedola (EA); Fiona Hanson (FH); Gareth Copley (GC); Gareth Fuller (GF); Gill Allen (GA); Hans Deryk (HD); Heathcliff O'Malley (HOM); Ian Vogler (IV); Ian West (IW); Jae C Hong (JCH); Jenny Goodall (JEG); Joe Giddens (JG); Joel Ryan (JR); John Giles (JOG); John Minchillo (JM); John Raoux (JR); John Stillwell (JS); Johnny Green (JGG); Jonathan Brady (JB); Kirsty Wigglesworth (KW); Lai Seng Sin (LSS); Leftaris Pitarakis (LP); Lewis Whyld (LW); Lionel Hahn (LH); Mario Tama (MAT); Mark Cuthbert (MC); Martin Keene (MK); Mary Turner (MT); Matt Crossick (MAC); Matt Dunham (MAD); Matt Rourke (MR); Michael Dunlea (MD); Michael Stephens (MS); Niall Carson (NC); Norman Parkinson (NP); Owen Humphreys (OW); PA News (PAN); Paul Rogers (PR); Phil Noble (PN); Press Association (PA); Rafiq Maqbool (RM); Rebecca Naden (RN); Richard Pohle (RP); Roger Allen (RA); Ron Bell (RB); Rui Vieira (RV); Samir Hussein (SH); Shaun Curry (SC); Sport and General (S&G); Stefan Rousseau (SR); Steve Parsons (SP); Sue Moore (SM); Suzanne Plunkett (SUP); Tim Graham (TG); Tim Ireland (TI); Tim Ockenden (TO); Tim Rooke (TR); Toby Melville (TM); Tom Hevezi (TH); Yui Mok (YM)

OTHER

One image, marked *, is courtesy of White House photographer Pete Souza and is in the public domain.